DORLING KINDERSLEY 📖 EYEWITNESS BOOKS

GORILLA,
MONKEY & APE

Mother mona
monkey and baby

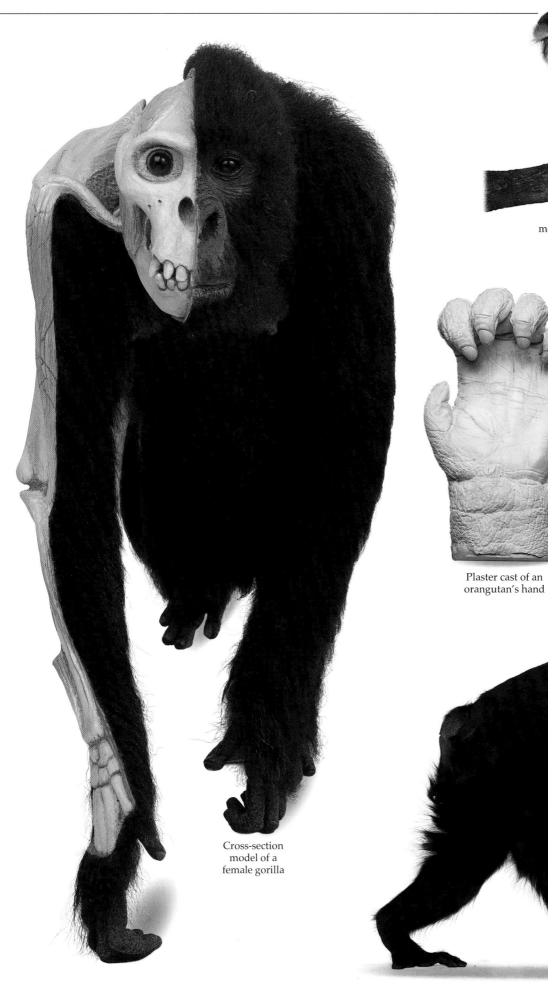

Cross-section
model of a
female gorilla

Plaster cast of an
orangutan's hand

Brown capuchin

Squirrel
monkey

DK EYEWITNESS BOOKS

GORILLA, MONKEY & APE

Written by
IAN REDMOND

Photographed by
PETER ANDERSON & GEOFF BRIGHTLING

Silverback
gorilla

Celebes
macaque

Skeleton hand
of an aye-aye

DK

Dorling Kindersley

Ring-tailed lemur

Dorling Kindersley
LONDON, NEW YORK, DELHI, JOHANNESBURG, MUNICH, PARIS and SYDNEY

For a full catalog, visit

DK www.dk.com

Female orangutan
and baby

Project editor Bridget Hopkinson
Editor Gin von Noorden
Art editor Andrew Nash
Managing editor Gillian Denton
Managing art editor Julia Harris
Researcher Céline Carez
Production Catherine Semark
Picture research Sarah Moule

This Eyewitness ® Book has been conceived by
Dorling Kindersley Limited and Editions Gallimard

© 1995 Dorling Kindersley Limited
This edition © 2000 Dorling Kindersley Limited
First American edition, 1995

Published in the United States by
Dorling Kindersley Publishing, Inc.
375 Hudson Street,
New York, NY 10014
4 6 8 10 9 7 5

Gorilla
skull

Dorling Kindersley books are available at special discounts for bulk purchases for sales
promotions or premiums. Special editions, including personalized covers, excerpts of
existing guides, and corporate imprints can be created in large quantities for specific
needs. For more information, contact Special Markets Dept., Dorling Kindersley
Publishing, Inc., 95 Madison Ave., New York, NY 10016; Fax: (800) 600-9098

Infant gorilla

Library of Congress Cataloging-in-Publication Data
Redmond, Ian.
   Gorilla, Monkey and Ape / written by Ian Redmond;
photography by Peter Anderson & Geoff Brightling.
   p. cm. — (Eyewitness Books)
   Includes index.
      1. Primates — Juvenile literature.
      [1. Gorilla. 2. Apes. 3. Monkeys. 4. Primates.]
      I. Anderson, Peter (Peter David), ill.
      II. Brightling, Geoff, ill. III. Title.
      QL737.P9R325   2000
      599.8—dc20   95–3241
      ISBN 0-7894-6037-8 (pb)
      ISBN 0-7894-6036-X (hc)

Color reproduction by Colourscan, Singapore
Printed in China by Toppan Printing Co. (Shenzhen) Ltd.

Silverback
gorilla

Patas monkey

Contents

Hamadryas
baboon

What are primates?

Chimpanzee

IT'S HARD TO IMAGINE that a mighty silverback gorilla (pp. 42–43) is related to the tiny mouse lemur (p. 10), but both of these animals are primates. They belong to a varied group of mammals that contains over 180 species. Primates can be divided into two broad groups: the anthropoids, which includes monkeys, apes, and humans; and the primitive primates, which includes lemurs, bush babies, and tarsiers. All primates share common features. Most species are tree-dwelling all or some of the time and their bodies are specially adapted for this way of life. Primates have forward-pointing eyes to help them judge the distances between branches and strong, gripping fingers that can hold on to tree trunks. However, the primates' most notable characteristic is their intelligence. Compared to their body sizes, they have relatively large brains. As a group, primates are clever and quick to learn new skills, making them arguably the most intelligent members of the animal kingdom.

Large braincase

A NOSE AHEAD
Most primitive primates, such as this black-and-white ruffed lemur (p. 10), have a long muzzle with a moist nose. Their highly developed sense of smell helps them to find food, detect scent markings on territorial boundaries, and sniff out danger.

Malar bone protects the eye

Eye socket faces slightly sideways

Long nasal bone sticks out between the eyes

Flatter nasal bone does not obstruct the eyes

Eye socket faces forward

EYES IN ORBIT
Placed on either side of its long muzzle, a lemur's eye sockets face slightly sideways. This gives the lemur a wider sphere of vision than a gorilla, but it also means that it cannot focus its eyes so well on a single object close at hand. Lemurs and other primitive primates such as bush babies therefore rely more on their senses of hearing and smell and tend to have longer noses and larger ears than the higher primates.

Smaller nose

Upper canine tooth

THE EYES HAVE IT
Monkeys and apes, or the higher primates, rely more on sight than on smell. The gorilla skull on the left shows how their eyes point forward to give overlapping fields of vision, allowing both eyes to focus on a single object. This provides excellent "stereoscopic vision," which enables the higher primates to judge distance and depth very accurately. Primates can also see in color.

Long, strong fingers can wrap around objects or grasp branches

Flat nail protects the sensitive pad of the fingertip

The palm supports objects held in the hand

Opposable thumb

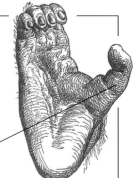

Opposable big toe

GRASPING TOES
A chimpanzee's (pp. 50–55) opposable big toe looks and works like a thumb. It can stretch out to form a strong, clamplike grip, allowing the chimp to dangle from a branch by one foot.

GENTLE GIANT
Although he is the most powerful of the great apes, an adult male gorilla can pick up a small grape without crushing it. His opposable thumb forms a precise and delicate grip with his forefinger, and his sensitive fingertips allow him to control the amount of pressure he uses. As with most primates, the gorilla's fingertips and toes are responsive to pressure and temperature and are protected by flat nails instead of claws.

HANDS OR FEET?
The feet of a chimpanzee look so similar to its hands that it is easy to see why 19th-century naturalists called apes and monkeys "quadrumana," or "four-handed" animals.

Plaster cast of an orangutan's (pp. 38–41) hand

FINGERS AND THUMBS
Most mammals have paws, hooves, or flippers that can do only one or two things, but a primate's hand is an extremely versatile instrument. Most primates have a special opposable thumb, a flexible thumb that can be pressed against the fingers to grip objects and tools precisely. The thumb can also be stretched out to grasp large branches.

HAND IN HAND
The similarity between a gorilla's hand and that of a human is striking. However, there are slight differences in shape because the hands are used for different tasks. A gorilla not only holds things with its hands, but also uses its knuckles for walking on (p. 8), so it has thick, sturdy fingers to support the weight of its upper body. Human hands are designed for holding tools and manipulating things, so the fingers are more delicate and the opposable thumb is longer.

Apes and humans

GREAT APES AND HUMANS belong to the same group of primates called the hominoids. Despite differences in limb length and jaw shape, the similarities between them can be seen in their bone structure. All hominoids have large skulls to house their big brains, and opposable thumbs (pp. 6–7) for gripping things. However, apes and humans are not directly related. Humans belong to a separate branch of the hominoid family called the hominids. This group includes modern humans (*Homo sapiens sapiens*) and our direct ancestors. Recent research suggests that the hominid and ape lines may have separated about seven million years ago.

A REVOLUTIONARY THEORY
This 19th-century cartoon shows the English naturalist Charles Darwin (1809–1882) portrayed as a monkey. He was lampooned for suggesting that animals, including apes and humans, evolved by a process of natural selection. People were outraged at the idea of sharing a common ancestor with a monkey.

DISTANT RELATION
Darwin noted that there were more differences between orangutans (pp. 38–41) and humans than between gorillas or chimps and humans. Unlike the other great apes, the orangutan (*Pongo pygmaeus*) spends most of its life in the trees and is specially adapted for this way of life. It spends much of its time literally hanging from branches: its long, powerful fingers and toes can easily carry its heavy body weight. The orangutan's extremely long arms also help it reach for fruit on high branches.

Long arm bone

Long, hooklike fingers for holding branches

Foot bends sideways when placed on the ground

BIG BROTHER
The gorilla (*Gorilla gorilla*) (pp. 42–49) is the second closest human relative. An adult male can grow to be as tall as a man, but may weigh almost as much as three men. Like the chimpanzee, the gorilla walks on its knuckles and has strong, sturdy bones to support its heavy weight. However, the gorilla is a gentle giant. Despite its awesome power, it is a peaceful vegetarian.

Sagittal crest forms an anchor for strong jaw muscles

Nuchal crest forms an anchor for powerful neck muscles

Large shoulder blade supports sturdy shoulder

Large jawbone

Ribcage wide at bottom

Opposable thumb

Opposable big toe

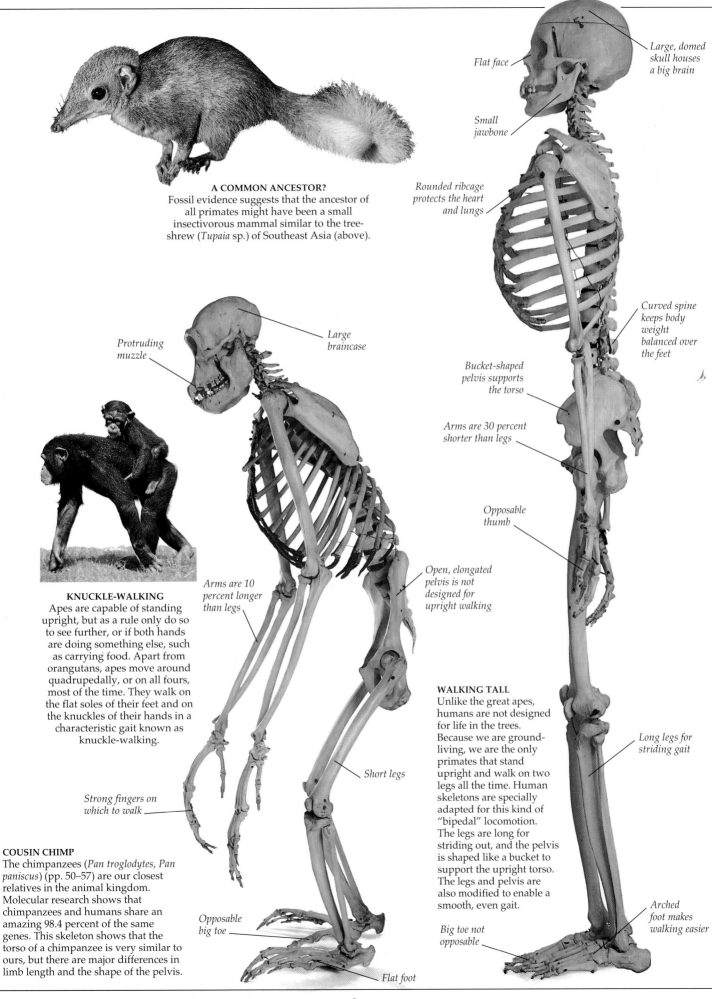

A COMMON ANCESTOR?
Fossil evidence suggests that the ancestor of all primates might have been a small insectivorous mammal similar to the tree-shrew (*Tupaia* sp.) of Southeast Asia (above).

Flat face

Large, domed skull houses a big brain

Small jawbone

Rounded ribcage protects the heart and lungs

Curved spine keeps body weight balanced over the feet

Protruding muzzle

Large braincase

Bucket-shaped pelvis supports the torso

Arms are 30 percent shorter than legs

Opposable thumb

KNUCKLE-WALKING
Apes are capable of standing upright, but as a rule only do so to see further, or if both hands are doing something else, such as carrying food. Apart from orangutans, apes move around quadrupedally, or on all fours, most of the time. They walk on the flat soles of their feet and on the knuckles of their hands in a characteristic gait known as knuckle-walking.

Arms are 10 percent longer than legs

Open, elongated pelvis is not designed for upright walking

Short legs

Strong fingers on which to walk

WALKING TALL
Unlike the great apes, humans are not designed for life in the trees. Because we are ground-living, we are the only primates that stand upright and walk on two legs all the time. Human skeletons are specially adapted for this kind of "bipedal" locomotion. The legs are long for striding out, and the pelvis is shaped like a bucket to support the upright torso. The legs and pelvis are also modified to enable a smooth, even gait.

Long legs for striding gait

COUSIN CHIMP
The chimpanzees (*Pan troglodytes, Pan paniscus*) (pp. 50–57) are our closest relatives in the animal kingdom. Molecular research shows that chimpanzees and humans share an amazing 98.4 percent of the same genes. This skeleton shows that the torso of a chimpanzee is very similar to ours, but there are major differences in limb length and the shape of the pelvis.

Opposable big toe

Flat foot

Big toe not opposable

Arched foot makes walking easier

Primitive primates

LEMURS, BUSH BABIES, LORISES, pottos, and tarsiers (pp. 12–13) are all primitive primates, or prosimians. Their bones resemble those of the first primates to evolve, which were probably small tree-dwellers similar to today's tree-shrews (p. 9). Although primitive primates have smaller brains than monkeys and apes, they are well adapted to the ecological niches, or conditions, in which they live. Lemurs are found only on the island of Madagascar in the Indian Ocean, where they have developed an interesting variety of feeding habits. Many lemurs eat fruit and leaves, but gentle lemurs (*Hapalemur* sp.) feed mainly on bamboo, and the mongoose lemur (*Lemur mongoz*) lives on nectar. The strangest lemur of all, the aye-aye, feeds like a woodpecker, prying out grubs from the bark of trees.

MADAGASCAR'S "MONKEYS"
This ring-tailed lemur (*Lemur catta*) is one of the 23 species of lemur found on Madagascar. The first lemurs reached Madagascar about 50 million years ago, but no one knows quite how they got there. They may have been carried across the sea from Africa clinging to fallen trees. With very few competing animals on Madagascar, the lemurs' descendants spread all over the island, filling a vast range of ecological niches.

NOISY RUFFIANS
Black-and-white ruffed lemurs (*Varecia variegata*) have incredibly loud voices – troops can hear each other at distances over half a mile (one kilometer) apart. Like all lemurs, ruffed lemurs are superb climbers. They scamper along sturdy branches, balancing with their long tails.

WORLD'S SMALLEST PRIMATE
The mouse lemur (*Microcebus murinus*) is so small it could sit on a human thumb – an adult might weigh only 1.5–3 oz (45–90 g). Mouse lemurs are considered the most primitive lemurs. They scurry around the branches in search of berries and insects, in much the same way ancestral primates did millions of years ago.

WARS OF THE NOSES
A striped tail is a useful fighting accessory. The bold markings, when held aloft, make a male's presence known to his enemies. As well as sending out visual signals, the tail can be used to send out strong scent signals too. Ring-tailed lemurs rub their tails with smelly secretions from their arm glands. When two rivals meet, they wave their tails in the air and fight a smelly duel, known as a "stink fight."

SMELLY ARMPITS

A sharp sense of smell is one of a lemur's most important assets. Between the elbow and wrist is a special gland, similar to the one that makes human armpits smell. Like a dog marking streetlamps, a lemur leaves lingering smells on branches as a way of passing information to other lemurs. This ring-tailed lemur is leaving its scent by brushing its forearms against a branch.

Middle finger has evolved into a special grub-picking tool

FINGER-LICKIN' GOOD

Because there are no woodpeckers on Madagascar, wood-boring beetle grubs have few predators. The aye-aye has evolved to exploit this handy food source – it uses its long middle finger and sharp, curved claw to pick out the fat grubs as they chew their tunnels in the wood.

Large ears pick up the sounds of the forest

Long muzzle and moist nose shows highly developed sense of smell

Sharp incisors for piercing through wood

CHISEL TEETH

Aye-ayes listen for the rustle of burrowing beetle grubs inside dead trees or branches, then use their strong incisor teeth to gnaw into the wood. They fish out the grubs with their long middle fingers, and tuck into a tasty meal. An aye-aye's front teeth grow all the time to make up for wear and tear.

LIFE IN A GROUP

Ring-tailed lemurs are gregarious social animals and live in troops of up to 30 members. They like nothing better than to start the day by sunning themselves and perhaps feeding on the blossoms of an agave plant.

Long tail wafts marking scents through the air

AYE-AYE?

The aye-aye (*Daubentonia madagascariensis*) is the most peculiar looking lemur. It has shaggy, dark-brown fur, large ears, and a pointed nose. It is rare on Madagascar, partly because the local people are superstitious about it. They believe that if they see an aye-aye and do not kill it, death will befall someone in their village.

LEAPING LEMURS

As big as an orangutan (pp. 38–41), the largest lemur, the "tratratratra," was wiped out by human settlers a few centuries ago. The largest lemur still alive in Madagascar is the indri (*Indri indri*) (right) – its name literally means "There it is!" in the local language. The indri leaps from tree to tree in astonishing, graceful bounds. It is camouflaged by black-and-white markings on its fur, which breaks up the animal's outline among the trees.

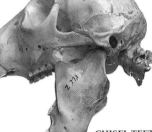

Primates of the night

In the dark of an african night, the quiet background of insect noises may be pierced by a strange, childlike cry. This is the call of the bush baby, or galago, a small, nocturnal primate. Bush babies have sensitive, mobile ears to detect moving insects, and large eyes to focus on their prey in moonlight or starlight. They are very agile, moving quickly and leaping from branch to branch. At the opposite end of the speed scale, but related to the galagos, are the lorises, the potto, and the angwantibo (*Arctocebus calabarensis*). These strange, slow primates are also nocturnal, and creep about the forest in search of fruit and creatures slow enough to be caught. There are no bush babies in Asia, but there is one fast-moving nocturnal primate – the tarsier. With their huge eyes, the three species of tarsier all look like tiny gremlins. In one species, a single eye weighs more than the animal's brain!

PRIMATE OWL
In spite of their large, appealing eyes and cute faces, tarsiers are efficient and ruthless predators. Hunting at night, they silently drop on to large insects, roosting birds, and even venomous snakes. They kill their prey with a nip of their sharp teeth, and meticulously finish off every edible morsel.

SLOW MOVER
A slender loris (*Loris tardigradus*) creeps through the trees, grasping branches with each hand and foot. Lorises eat the slow-moving caterpillars, beetles, and millipedes that faster insectivores leave behind.

Second finger is only a small bump

A LEAP IN THE DARK
The nocturnal spectral tarsier (*Tarsius spectrum*) is only the size of a squirrel, yet it can leap across gaps of 20 ft (6 m). Tarsiers spend most of their lives holding on to and jumping between upright stems. With their tails as props, they can even sleep clinging to vertical branches.

Enlarged thumb

PINCER FINGERS
This plaster cast of a potto's (*Perodicticus potto*) hand shows how its muscular thumb is set at 180 degrees opposite the other fingers. The hand works just like a pincer, allowing the potto to grasp branches and small trees in a clamplike grip.

Pincer-shaped hand can close tightly around branches

Rounded cranium, or braincase

Postorbital bar protects side of eye

ALL EYES
The main feature of a loris's face are its eyes. Enormous orbits, or eyesockets, are set into the skull and protected by a thick, bony ring called the orbital margin.

CRUNCHY SUPPER
This lesser bush baby (*Galago senegalensis*) is eating a praying mantis. After spending the day asleep, a bush baby sets off to hunt as soon as it is dark. Its large, mobile ears are sensitive to the sounds made by insects, scorpions, spiders, lizards, or nesting birds. Bush babies also eat fallen fruit, petals, nectar, and the sap of some trees.

Large, mobile ears for detecting movement of prey

Enormous eyes for keen night vision

SCENT SIGNALS
This greater bush baby's (*Galago crassicaudatus*) powerful back legs suggest that it is a vertical clinger and leaper, like a tarsier. But scientists have found that different bush baby species move in different ways – some move on all fours, while others seldom leap at all. However they move about their territory, bush babies let others know of their presence by annointing their hands and feet with their own urine. In this way, every handhold and foothold leaves a smelly message saying "I was here."

Long, powerful legs for gripping and for leaping from branch to branch

Hand has six protective pads on palm

Arms are relatively short, with hands for grabbing prey

Marmosets and tamarins

FEEL THE WAY
Marmosets such as this tassel-ear marmoset (*Callithrix humeralifer*) have long bristles on their wrists to help them feel the branches.

WITH THEIR PUNK HAIRSTYLES and bright colors, marmosets and tamarins are among the most attractive primates on earth. These fast-moving, lightweight animals live in the rainforests of South America. Their small size makes it easy for them to dart about the trees, catching insects and small animals such as lizards, frogs, and snails. Marmosets have another unusual food source – they use their chisel-like incisor teeth to dig into tree bark and lap up the gummy sap that seeps out, leaving telltale, oval-shaped holes in the branches when they have finished. But as vast tracts of rainforest are cleared for plantations and cattle ranches, marmosets and tamarins are in serious danger of extinction.

LEAP FOR LIFE
The saddle-back tamarin (*Saguinus fuscicollis*) is about 1 ft (30 cm) long, with a tail of the same length. Like all marmosets and tamarins, its small size makes it an easy meal for sharp-eyed birds of prey. Its best defense is a great leap, using its long tail as a rudder. Saddle-backs often feed in mixed troops with emperor tamarins (*Saguinus imperator*), in order to increase the number of eyes on the lookout for danger.

LUCKY LION
The golden lion tamarin (*Leontopithecus rosalia*) is in danger of extinction, but breeds well in captivity. Many zoo-bred animals have been released back into the coastal forests of eastern Brazil, their original habitat.

Long white crest makes tamarin easy to spot among thick jungle foliage

A tamarin grooms its tail by holding the tip with one hand and scratching it with the claws of the other hand

Sensitive nose roots out juicy fruits and insects

Sharp claws instead of fingernails for grooming

Long fingers for gripping branches

COTTON-TOP CREW
With their punky white crests, cotton-top tamarins (*Saguinus oedipus*) have a striking appearance. They are in great demand for the pet trade, which has led to a rapid decline of numbers in their native Colombian forests. In the wild, tamarins live in extended family groups of up to 15 individuals. They are very affectionate and spend much of their time grooming each other with their claws.

ON THE LOOKOUT
Marmosets and tamarins normally move around on all fours, running along and jumping from one branch to the next. If they want a better view, they simply stand on their hind legs like this red-handed tamarin (*Saguinus midas*).

Father keeps a sharp eye on his surroundings

UNCOMMON CREATION
This strange-looking creature is a
19th-century artist's impression
of a common marmoset
(*Callithrix jacchus*).

ROLE REVERSAL
This silvery marmoset
(*Callithrix argentata*) family
is not what it seems – the
adult is not the babies'
mother! In marmoset and
tamarin families, the father
does most of the work,
carrying and caring for the
babies from birth to weaning.
The female usually carries her
young only when she is
suckling them. For marmosets
and tamarins, twins are the
rule rather than the exception.
The twins are not identical
because they come from
separate eggs, and so could
be either male and female
or two of the same sex.

*Twins cling to
their father's thick
fur as he moves
through the trees*

*Claws allow marmoset
to climb a vertical tree
trunk without slipping*

*Babies only clamber off
their father's back to be
fed by their mother*

*Hole cut by front teeth of
marmoset feeding on
gum under bark*

SMALL SNACK
The pygmy marmoset
(*Cebuella pygmaea*) is the
smallest New World primate.
A mere 3 oz (85 g), it is
nevertheless a tasty snack for
predators. To avoid birds of
prey, it spends most of its
time on the lower tree
trunks. Marmosets
are partial to tree
sap, which they collect
by gouging into edible tree
bark with their sharp teeth.

*Tail used as a
brace against
trunk*

New World monkeys

NEW WORLD MONKEYS live in the lush jungles of Central and South America. Unlike their Old World relatives (pp. 22–25), they are entirely tree-dwelling and are well adapted to this way of life. Many, such as howler, spider, and woolly monkeys, have semi- or fully prehensile tails (pp. 18–19) that wrap around branches like an extra limb. Others, such as the sakis and uakaris, have extraordinary leaping abilities; the titi has strong, grasping feet; and the tiny squirrel monkey can scamper along even the smallest branches. In contrast to Old World monkeys, New World monkeys have broad, sideways-pointing nostrils and no sitting pads.

NEW WORLD HABITATS
Monkeys probably colonized South America over 40 million years ago, when the land was closer to Africa. They have spread as far as southern Mexico in Central America.

White face patch shows up in moonlight

Large eyes for seeing at night

Crouching position typical of New World monkeys, which lack sitting pads

THE OWL MONKEY
Most unusual of the New World monkeys is the douroucouli, also called the night or owl monkey (*Aotus trivirgatus*), the world's only nocturnal monkey. During the day, douroucoulis sleep in hollow trees or thick vegetation, but as night falls, they come out to forage for fruit, leaves, and insects. The male hoots by the light of the moon to proclaim his territory and to locate his female. Douroucoulis mate for life and the father is the main child-rearer.

Long, bushy tail acts as a counterweight for balancing

TREETOP TRAVELER
The black-bearded saki always travels through the trees on all fours, making huge leaps when it reaches the end of a branch.

STEALTHY TREE STALKER
Snakes are a constant threat to arboreal, or tree-dwelling, monkeys. South America is home to two of the world's largest snake species, the boa constrictor (above) and the anaconda. The aquatic anaconda usually snatches monkeys that venture too near a river, although it can also climb trees. The boa, however, spends all its time lurking in the treetops, waiting to trap unwary animals in its deadly coils.

Wide, sideways-pointing nostrils characteristic of New World monkeys

BUSHY BEARD
The black-bearded saki (*Chiropotes satanas*) lives high in the upper canopy of the rainforest and feeds mainly on seeds, with some fruit and insects. Its bushy beard hides a powerful jaw with special incisor teeth for cracking open tough-shelled fruit and nuts. The dark, brooding appearance of the black-bearded saki led to its other name – the satan monkey.

Bald uakari
(*Cacajao calvus*)

RED-FACED LEAPER
Even though they lack long tails for balancing or gripping, the uakaris of the Amazon basin are expert tree-climbers. They are among the best leapers in the forest and often swing from branches or hang by their feet to feed on fruit. Despite their angry-looking red faces, uakaris are shy, unaggressive monkeys.

Branches marked with a "scent-trail" from scent on monkey's fur

Flexible tail curls around branch for support

SCAMPERING SQUIRREL
The common squirrel monkey (*Saimiri sciureus*) is found in almost every South American rainforest. These light, nimble monkeys scamper through the trees like squirrels, following familiar scent-marked pathways in the forest canopy. Squirrel monkeys live and travel in large groups that can number up to 200 animals. They are often accompanied by brown capuchins (pp. 20–21), both species gaining protection from increased numbers.

WRAP UP
When squirrel monkeys are sitting, they often wrap their long, flexible tails around their shoulders.

Quick fingers can snatch insects

Agile squirrel monkey performs amazing acrobatic feats high in the forest canopy

Tail used as an anchor

White-handed titi (*Callicebus torquatus*)

Extra-strong hands and feet for gripping

Titi often entwines its tail with its mate's

THE TITI
Titis are small, noisy monkeys that feed on fruit and insects. Males and females mate for life and live in small family groups with their offspring. The father is the main child-rearer and cares for his young well into adolescence.

BALANCING ACT
Little squirrel monkeys are light enough to climb out onto thin branches that would break under the weight of larger monkeys. This enables them to reach tasty fruit and flowers that have been left untouched by other species. Squirrel monkeys are omnivorous, living on a mixed diet of plant and animal foods. They spend many hours foraging for fruit in the forest canopy, but their preferred food is insects.

Life in the treetops

IN THE NEW WORLD forests, there are 17 species of monkey that have a prehensile tail – a fabulous feature that is particularly useful for life in the treetops. Not found on any other primate, prehensile tails are strong and muscular and can be used to grasp branches and objects. They also have sensitive tips, which means that they function almost like an extra hand.

A monkey with a prehensile tail can suspend itself from a tree by its tail alone. This is very useful when gathering fruit or leaves that would otherwise be out of reach on weak twigs at the end of a branch. Access to this plentiful supply of food has enabled these "five-handed" monkeys to evolve a large body size. The biggest monkey in South America is the woolly spider monkey (*Brachyteles arachnoides*), which weighs up to 22 lbs (10 kg).

CURLICUE TAIL
This 19th-century engraving of a woolly monkey is misleading. Its tail rarely curls in the air – instead, its owner wraps it around the nearest branch.

GET A GRIP
New World monkeys have a bare patch of skin at the end of their tails, like a tiny palm of a hand. It is very sensitive, gives a good grip, and even has a pattern of ridges like fingerprints.

ARTISTIC LICENSE
Spider monkeys don't really have three arms – the artist who painted this changed his mind about the position of the monkey's arm, and painted a branch instead!

Heavily built howler moves slowly through the branches and rarely leaps

Prehensile tail is used as an anchor

Red howler monkey
(*Alouetta seniculus*)

LOUD MOUTH
Howler monkeys certainly live up to their name. Their howls, which are more like roars, echo through the forests at dawn, marking out their territory to other monkey troops. Both male and female howler monkeys have a deep jaw with a special egg-shaped chamber to amplify their calls.

There are six species of howler monkey and they are one of the most widespread New World monkeys.

BLACK-HAND GANG
This black-handed spider monkey (*Ateles geoffroyi*) lives in forests from southern Mexico to northwestern Colombia. It is one of four recognized spider monkey species, all of which have a number of sub-species. Spider monkeys have an appropriate name. They clamber around the canopy with their "five" limbs like a spider moving around its web. Unlike howlers, agile spider monkeys sometimes make long leaps down to the branches below.

Muscular prehensile tail carries most of monkey's weight

Underside of tail is packed with sweat glands and nerve endings

Common woolly monkey
(*Lagothrix lagotricha*)

WOOLLY SWINGERS
This woolly monkey is as adept at running along branches on all fours as it is swinging beneath them. Woolly monkeys live in groups of 20 or more. They crash through the jungle canopy, the lighter-colored babies hanging on to any part of their mothers' bodies. Woolly monkeys have very muscular tails – one captive male, hanging from a rope by his tail, playfully lifted a man off the ground!

Four long fingers form a hooklike grip

Spider monkeys lack thumbs on their hands

Arms are extremely long and flexible

SIPPING SPIDERS
Spider monkeys are fruit eaters whose flexible society allows the size of the group to vary according to how much fruit is available. If large fruit trees are in season, gangs of up to 20 monkeys join up temporarily, but if food is scarce, they forage singly or in small groups. Spider monkeys prefer ripe fruit, but eat some foliage too – the monkey on the left is sipping water from a balsa flower high up in the canopy.

JUICY FRUIT
The fragrant passion fruit (*Passiflora edulis*) is a delicious treat for New World monkeys. Because the seeds are embedded in the juicy flesh, the monkeys consume them as well, thereby helping to distribute the seeds – when they pass through the monkey's gut, they fall to the forest floor a long way from the parent plant.

Short, thick fur

Baby clings on tightly

TREETOP NURSERY
A spider monkey has a single baby, which is born after a gestation (see p. 48) of about 139 days. For the first four months, the baby clings on to the mother's belly, but later it rides on her back. The infant often curls its prehensile tail around its mother's tail to hang on tight – one slip could mean a fatal fall of more than 100 ft (30 m).

Toes are long and flexible

Black spider monkey
(*Ateles paniscus*)

The clever capuchin

CAPUCHINS ARE FOUND IN ALMOST EVERY South American forest. The brown, black-capped, or tufted, capuchin (*Cebus apella*) is the most widely ranging New World monkey. It is also the most intelligent, which may account for its ability to adapt to conditions in many different areas. Compared to its body size, the brain of the capuchin is relatively large. Its ingenuity and tool-using skills have led some scientists to describe the capuchin as the "South American chimpanzee." These accomplished monkeys are also known as "organ-grinder monkeys," because their talent for learning tricks made them a favorite with organ grinders (p. 60). However, the capuchin's cleverness sometimes brings it into conflict with humans. Bands of up to 30 monkeys often raid crops, outwitting farmers' efforts to keep them out. Such large numbers can consume vast amounts of food in a short time, which naturally makes them unpopular with their human neighbors.

Brown capuchin

Tail can be used to hold fruit

BANANA RAIDER
This white-throated capuchin (*Cebus capucinus*) is stealing bananas, running on two legs so it can carry as much fruit in its arms as possible. It will take its stolen prize to a safe eating place.

Cap of dark fur like a monk's hood

Bright, alert eyes

Body weighs about 5 lbs (2.2 kg)

CAPUCHINS OF THE CANOPY
The capuchin gets its name from the cap of black fur on its head, which resembles a Franciscan monk's cowl or "capuche." It spends most of its time in the forest canopy, but sometimes comes down to the ground during the day. Capuchins live in mixed groups of between six and 30 animals, who spread out when foraging for food in the treetops. The dominant male and those he allows close to him usually occupy the best feeding positions, with low-ranking members banished to the edge of the group. Here they keep an eye out for predators such as the deadly harpy eagle.

Capuchin scampers easily along the branches of the forest canopy

FOREST FEAST
Capuchins eat a wide variety of fruits, which make up about 60 percent of their diet. They are also adept at catching insects and small animals such as lizards, young birds, squirrels, and even smaller species of monkey.

NUT-CRACKER
The brown capuchin loves palm nuts. Like the chimpanzee, it has learned how to crack open nuts using a variety of techniques (pp. 54–55). With its tail firmly anchored to a tree, the capuchin slams the nut against either a branch or another nut to crack it. This method, known as "proto-tool use," is also used by seashore-dwelling capuchins to open shellfish on rocks.

Capuchins usually feed and rest in a squatting position

Long, agile fingers are ideal for manipulating objects

Semi-prehensile tail (p. 18) used as an anchor in the trees

Old World monkeys

OLD WORLD AREAS
This map shows the distribution of monkeys throughout Asia and Africa. In the past, Asia and Africa were called the "Old World" because they were known to Europeans long before the "discovery" of the Americas, or "New World," in the 15th century. Today, the monkeys from these different continents are still referred to by these old-fashioned names.

T HE MONKEYS OF ASIA AND AFRICA, the so-called "Old World," form the largest and most varied group of primates. Despite their many differences, baboons, guenons, macaques, mangabeys, colobus, and leaf monkeys all belong to one zoological family, the Cercopithecidae. A typical Old World monkey has close-set, downward-pointing nostrils, sitting pads, and a non-prehensile tail (p. 18). Old World monkeys live in almost every kind of habitat, from the mangrove swamps of Borneo to the mountain forests of Asia and the plains of Africa. They also have a wide variety of diets and lifestyles. Some monkeys spend most of their lives in the treetops, eating only fruit and leaves, while others live both in the trees and on the ground, feeding on a mixed diet of plants, insects, and small animals. In general, monkeys with a more varied diet tend to be more ingenious and adaptable than plant-eaters.

Male group leader

Baboon keeps a lookout for predators between sips of water

Sitting pads, or ischial callosities

Bent tail is characteristic of baboons

SHY LION
Not only does the lion-tailed macaque (p. 28) have a tail like a lion, it also has an impressive mane of gray hair, which is intended to make it look bigger. But despite its ferocious appearance, this monkey is a shy forest-dweller, unlike its more boisterous macaque relatives.

BOTTOMS UP
Unlike New World monkeys, all Old World monkeys, such as the olive baboon (p. 27), have sitting pads of hard skin called ischial callosities. Old World monkeys sleep sitting up, and their ischial callosities enable them to rest their weight on their bottoms quite comfortably.

Downward-pointing nostrils

Bright yellow eyebrows

TREE-DWELLING TROOP
The mona monkey (*Cercopithecus mona*) is typical of Africa's forest guenons, the most common group of African monkeys. Monas live in troops of up to 20 monkeys led by one dominant male. They run and leap through the trees, feeding on leaves, fruit, and insects. The male proclaims his presence to neighboring troops with a loud "eeow" call, made louder with the help of a small throat sac. Occasionally, mona monkeys join together with other species of monkey at a plentiful food source, finding extra protection in numbers.

Mother suckling baby

Blue face, characteristic of some guenons

Startling rings of pale skin around the eyes can be seen from a distance in the forest

WHO NOSE?
The proboscis monkey (*Nasalis larvatus*) is one of the strangest-looking Old World monkeys. The adult males have enormous, drooping noses that can measure up to 3 in (7.6 cm). Scientists are not sure why the male proboscis has such a large nose, but it may be to attract females. This extraordinary monkey is also unusual because it likes to swim. Proboscis monkeys live in the mangrove swamps of Borneo and have been known to dive into water from heights of up to 50 ft (15 m).

THERE LIES A TAIL
The rare golden langur (*Presbytis geei*) lives in the forests of northwest Assam, India. Like other species of langur, it has an extra-long tail, from which it gets its name – "lungoor" means "long tail" in Hindustani.

The proboscis monkey feeds on the young leaves of mangrove trees

WHAT A SPECTACLE
This dusky leaf monkey (*Presbytis obscura*) acquires its striking white spectacles at about six weeks old. Also known as langurs, leaf monkeys live throughout southern Asia. Because their diets consist mainly of leaves, these unusual monkeys have special four-chambered stomachs that contain bacteria to digest the plant fiber.

23

Continued on next page

Treetop runners

Although extremely agile, Old World monkeys do not swing through the trees like some of their New World cousins (pp. 16–19). Instead, they walk or run along the tops of branches, traveling on well-known pathways through the treetops. When a monkey reaches the end of a branch, it often makes a death-defying leap to the next tree. While airborne, a leaping monkey holds out its arms and legs and uses its tail as a rudder to control its "flight." After it lands in the next tree, the monkey hangs on to its swaying support and quickly recovers its balance before scampering off.

Baby's tail wrapped tightly around its mother

Cape of long white hairs spreads out as the monkey leaps between branches

Strong back legs for leaping

Long, tassled tail acts as a rudder in mid-flight

Baby must hold on tight to its mother's fur or risk death by falling to the ground

Even carrying an infant, the mona monkey (p. 23) runs swiftly and easily along the branch

HIGH FLYER
Like the langurs of Asia (p. 23), African colobus monkeys can survive almost entirely on leaves, and rarely come down to the ground. The black-and-white colobus, or guereza (*Colobus guereza*), lives high in the forest canopy and is a fearless sky-diver, often diving down 30 ft (9 m) to lower-level trees. These beautiful monkeys have long been hunted for their spectacular coats, but they are now protected by law.

Mangabeys can communicate by raising their eyebrows like macaques (pp. 28–29)

Black crest flattens when the monkey raises its eyebrows

Long tail used for balance

Long, gray whiskers hide cheek pouches for storing food

Hollow cheeks are a common mangabey feature

AMAZING MANGABEYS
Mangabeys are large, striking-looking monkeys that live in the tropical rainforests of Africa. The black-crested mangabey (*Cerocebus aterrimus*) (left) lives in the forest canopy and rarely comes down to the ground, but the golden-bellied mangabey (*Cerocebus galeritus*) (right) often spends time foraging on the forest floor.

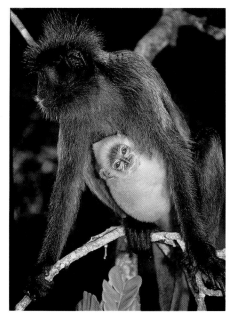

Small, neat ears
attuned to the
sounds of the forest

Baby mona monkey
is a perfect, tiny
replica of its mother

BRINGING UP BABY

The silvered leaf monkey (*Presbytis cristata*),
found in forests from Myanmar to Borneo, is
one of seven species of leaf monkey (p. 23) to
have bright orange babies. The infants' coats
contrast vividly with the darker fur of the
adults and last until they are about three
months old. This remarkable color difference
is thought to be linked to the leaf monkey's
unusual group behavior. When a baby is
born, it is inspected and groomed by every
female in the group. The baby's bright color
may act as a signal to evoke this caring
attention. Later, groups of youngsters are
looked after by a female "babysitter" while
their mothers forage for food.

MARKED FOR SUCCESS

There are about 20 species of guenon
throughout Africa. Famous for their distinctive
facial markings, guenons can be found in
numerous habitats. The handsome De Brazza's
monkey (*Cercopithecus neglectus*) (below), is a shy
forest-dweller, while the more common green
guenon (*Cercopithecus aethiops*) (right), also
known as the grass, grivet, vervet, or tantalus
monkey, lives on the African plains (p. 26).

Tail held erect
during male
dominance display

Chestnut-colored
"tiara"

White
beard will
grow longer

White stripe
becomes more
pronounced
with age

Each hair has bands
of different colors,
giving the coat a
brindled look

Long tail is
vulnerable
to damage

Life on the plains

SOME OLD WORLD MONKEYS have adapted to living on the grassy savannas and rocky plateaus of Africa. Life in these exposed, often harsh, habitats is difficult and often dangerous, for the savannas, or plains, are also home to predators such as lions, leopards, cheetahs, and hyenas. Lone monkeys would have little chance of survival, so they band together in close-knit groups for protection. Savanna-dwellers also need to be extremely tough and resourceful, and they are quick to take advantage of new food sources. They supplement their diet of grass and seeds with almost anything else they can lay their hands on, and baboons have even learned how to hunt hares and young gazelles.

MAGNIFICENT MONKEY
This 17th-century engraving shows the male hamadryas baboon's impressive cape of hair that hangs around its shoulders. The cape gives the baboon a regal bearing, and this large, powerfully built monkey has been admired since around 3000 B.C. (p. 58) for its strength and resilience.

THE VERSATILE VERVET
The vervet (*Cercopithecus aethiops*) is the most common monkey on the African plains. Like the other plains primates, it is equally at home in the trees as on the ground. Apart from savanna grass and seeds, vervets live on the gum and bark of the acacia tree, and they have special cheek pouches in which to store food.

Distinctive russet red coat

Long, distinguished-looking whiskers

Long legs for sprinting over the savanna

Monkey stands on its hind legs when alarmed

Baby clings tightly to mother's abdomen

LIFE ON THE RUN
The African savanna is a dangerous place, and monkeys like this female patas are always on the lookout for predators such as lions or leopards. Even when carrying a baby, a female patas can run fast over a long distance if need be. At night, patas monkeys sleep in the relative safety of the acacia trees that grow on the plains.

PLAINS COMMANDER
The patas monkey (*Erythrocebus patas*) is also known as the military monkey because of its distinguished appearance. The male's red coat and long, military-looking mustache make him look like a 19th-century army colonel. On the plains, the male patas lives up to his gentlemanly reputation: patas monkeys live in groups of up to 20 females with one male group leader whose job is to keep a lookout and to protect the females from danger. He does this by acting as a decoy. If the male spots an approaching predator, he makes a lot of noise and leads the predator away from the group. Patas monkeys can escape danger by sprinting at speeds of up to 35 mph (55 kmh).

Sharp canine

MIGHTY MOUTH
This olive baboon (*Papio anubis*) is showing his teeth to warn off an opponent. Male baboons often have skirmishes to establish their rank in the troop's hierarchy. The dominant males are responsible for maintaining the strict discipline that is vital for the troop's survival.

A PRIMATE PREDATOR
Baboons are not only preyed upon, they also can be predators themselves. These large, strong monkeys sometimes team up to hunt young gazelles. Fresh meat is a welcome addition to their diet of grass, seeds, fruit, roots, and insects.

The "groomer" picks out parasites and bits of dirt from the other's fur

KEEPING IT IN THE FAMILY
Most species of baboon live in large troops of mixed sexes and age-groups supervised by several adult males. However, the hamadryas baboon (*Papio hamadryas*) has a different arrangement. Females such as this one, live in small groups, called harems, of up to 12 members, which are governed by just one adult male. The male guards his females jealously and will chase after individuals that stray too far away. At night, many harems band together for safe sleeping on cliffs or rocky outcrops.

Cheek pouch used as a "shopping bag" for storing food

Olive-gray fur blends in with a background of rocks and dry grasses

SOOTHING INFLUENCE
The aggressive baboon also has a gentle side to its nature. Like many other primates, baboons spend a large amount of time peacefully grooming each other. Apart from helping the baboons to keep clean, this activity strengthens social bonds in an environment where group cooperation is vital for survival.

Doglike muzzle

Bony ridge protects the eyes

Hands used for picking grass and digging up roots

Bright red sitting pads (p. 22)

Strong legs for walking long distances

The versatile macaque

MACAQUES ARE THE MOST WIDESPREAD group of primates apart from humans. They can be found in almost every kind of habitat, in countries as far apart as Morocco, Afghanistan, India, and Japan. Macaques are successful at survival because they are extremely versatile. Most of the 15 species live and feed both on the ground and in the trees. They will eat almost anything, and new feeding habits are copied and learned by all the members of a troop. This adaptable behavior has allowed macaques to populate such diverse places as tropical forests, snowy mountains, and town garbage dumps.

THE UPWARDLY MOBILE MONKEY
The lion-tailed macaque (*Macaca silenus*) is a good example of macaque adaptability. By spending most of its time high up in the trees, it avoids direct competition with the bonnet macaque (*Macaca radiata*) that lives on the forest floor. However, the lion-tailed macaque is now confined to the dense mountain forests of southwest India and has become an endangered species.

Cheek pouches can be filled with food to be eaten later

Upright crest flattens when macaque raises its eyebrows, giving emphasis to its expression

THE BIG BOSS
The macaque troop is ruled by a dominant older male, who settles disputes, protects the group from attack, and leads the way to new feeding sites. The dominant male always takes the best feeding position and will not allow others near him until he has had his fill. He threatens unruly adolescents that come too close by staring, grunting, or biting if the offender is persistent.

Ischial callosities

Older male has grayish fur

YOUNG MALE
A young male macaque such as this one reaches maturity at about four and a half years old, although he will keep growing until he is about 10. Whereas juvenile females stay in the group with their mothers, young males have to leave and join a neighboring group.

Dominant male macaque weighs about 22 lbs (10 kg)

28

CURLY TAIL
The pig-tailed macaque (*Macaca nemestrina*) is a stocky monkey that lives in the forests of Southeast Asia. Some coconut-pickers use pig-tailed macaques to harvest coconuts (p. 61) because they are strong and can easily learn new skills.

Short, curly tail

JACUZZI LIFESTYLE
Japanese macaques (*Macaca fuscata*) have made some amazing adaptations to cope with their harsh environment in the mountains of Honshu. During the winter they eat seeds and the bark off trees, grow thicker coats, and cluster together to keep warm. However, one group has developed the remarkable habit of bathing in hot springs. Scientists studying the group were amazed to see a youngster jumping into the warm water. Other monkeys soon followed, and the behavior spread to become a regular winter pastime.

Adult female weighs around 11 lbs (5 kg)

Macaques communicate with a variety of facial expressions

Lack of tail means Celebes macaques are often mistakenly called apes

Juvenile female stays close to her mother

Newborn baby has pink skin

Older infant has dark skin

Baby is carried ventrally, or underneath its mother

Macaque walks on flat feet and palms of hands with extended fingers and toes

Macaque society

Celebes macaques (*Macaca nigra*) are born into a complex society with many rules. Infants stay close to their mothers and learn from their behavior about the group's hierarchy. The status of a young macaque is determined by the status of its mother until it is old enough to become established in the group. Once socially experienced, a macaque remembers which infant belongs to which mother and treats them accordingly. Behavior that is essential for survival is also quickly learned – new feeding patterns are soon copied by all group members, making the macaque one of the most versatile of all monkeys.

King swingers

In the forests of southern Asia, the early morning air is filled with the extraordinary sound of singing gibbons. The chorus of loud whoops and shrieks is the gibbons' way of proclaiming their territories to their neighbors. A pair of gibbons will defend roughly 60 acres (25 hectares) of rainforest, enough to provide a year-round supply of fruit. Although they could be mistaken for monkeys, gibbons are actually small apes. The nine species of gibbon are known as the lesser apes, because they are distinctly different from the great apes (pp. 36–37). They are much smaller and spend their entire lives in the trees. Unlike great apes, gibbons do not build nests, because they sleep sitting upright on branches, resting on their tough ischial callosities (p. 22). Gibbons are the only true "brachiators" among the apes. This means that they can swing hand over hand through the trees.

Hand reaches out for next branch

Extra-long arm

Broad shoulders

Shaggy black fur

Short leg

DAWN DIVA
In the early morning and late afternoon, pairs of gibbons sing loud duets to warn other couples to stay out of their territories. The male gives simple hoots, but the female sings the major part of the song, known as her "great call." It begins with a melodious whooping and climaxes in a high-pitched, bubbling sound. Calls of response from neighboring females soon join in, filling the air with a noisy chorus.

SINGING SIAMANG
The siamang (*Hylobates syndactylus*) of Malaysia and Sumatra is the biggest and loudest of the gibbons. It is equipped with a special throat sac to enhance its call. The inflated sac produces an astonishing booming sound that resonates through the forest, accompanied by a series of high-pitched whistles and barks. Siamangs can share the same territory as other gibbons, but they are partly leaf-eaters and so do not compete for much of the forest fruit.

Gibbons travel through the trees by brachiating, which means hanging below the branches and swinging from hand to hand. The motion of their arms resembles the left-right motion of striding legs.

During brachiation, a gibbon hangs from one hand like a pendulum while swinging its body around to allow the other hand to grasp the next handhold. A gibbon's elongated arms make for long swings.

When brachiating slowly, a gibbon reaches out for a new grip while holding on with the other hand. But at speed, it often lets go between handholds, flying briefly through the air before grasping another branch.

OUT-OF-REACH TREAT

The tastiest young leaves, buds, and fruits generally grow on twigs at the ends of branches, well out of reach of most animals. Gibbons have a small enough body weight, under 13 lbs (6 kg), and a long enough armspan, up to 5 ft (1.5 m), to be able to hang from the strongest part of a branch but still reach the twigs where food grows. This kind of eating habit is called "terminal branch feeding."

Hooklike fingers hang on to branch

SWINGING NEST

A baby gibbon is born naked except for a furry cap on its head, so it depends entirely on its mother for warmth. She bends her knees up to her stomach to make a warm, furry nest for her baby (below). However, the baby must support itself in its warm cradle by gripping tightly to the mother's fur as she swings through the trees high above the ground.

GIBBON FAMILY

Gibbons live in family groups made up of two parents and up to four offspring. A baby is born after a seven- to eight-month gestation period (p. 48) and is weaned early in its second year. Another baby is usually born two to three years after the first. The young do not leave their parents until the age of six or seven, so it is common to see families like these lar gibbons (*Hylobates lar*), with two or three offspring.

Elbow can be fully extended for swinging

THE WRIST TWIST

The bones of a gibbon's wrist are unique. Almost like a ball-and-socket joint in composition, they allow the gibbon to rotate its body as it swings without loosening its grip. A gibbon's shoulders also have a wider range of movement than other apes and monkeys. Its body trunk is broader from side to side than from front to back.

Thick, fluffy fur

Mother raises her knees to support her baby

Tiny fingers can grip tightly

The drawback with high-speed brachiation is that a dead or slender branch, grabbed in haste, can sometimes snap. Studies show that a surprising number of gibbons suffer broken bones from falls.

Ischial callosities (p. 22)

Expert communicators

ALTHOUGH PROSIMIANS, MONKEYS, AND APES cannot talk like humans, they have many subtle and complex ways of communicating with each other. Primates use a combination of facial expressions, gestures, markings, sounds, and scents to convey a wide range of information. In a group, it is vital to know if food has been found or when danger is near, but it is also important to observe social signals. Annoying the dominant male could lead to a painful bite, so youngsters learn how to identify threatening gestures such as staring, showing the teeth, or slapping the ground. On the other hand, they also need to recognize an invitation to groom or play, which could be signified by lip-smacking, a friendly look, or a "play face." In dense forests, it is harder to detect visual signals, so sounds and scents play an important role. Some monkeys and apes use loud calls to proclaim their territories or to attract a mate. In a quieter way, scent markings do the same thing. Whatever the message, there is no doubt that primates are expert communicators.

WHAT'S GOING ON?
A young chimpanzee expresses anxiety by bristling its hair and making a soft "hoo" sound, building up to a series of whimpers, through pouting lips. Its mother will respond with a reassuring hug. A rising "hoo," without pouting, means "what's that?" and other chimps will come to investigate.

GRIN AND BARE IT
When a chimp is frightened or excited, it warns others by making a "fear grin," flashing its pink gums and white teeth in a distinctive signal. If the chimp is involved in a fight or trying to scare off a predator, a fear grin might be accompanied by shrieks and screams.

Teeth are covered by upper lip in open-mouthed "play face"

HAPPY TALK
Rather like people, chimpanzees use a combination of facial expressions and vocalizations to communicate their feelings to other members of the group (pp. 52–53). These two young chimps are play-fighting, and their high spirits are signified by open-mouthed "play faces" and cheerful laughing noises.

COLOR CODE
The mandrill (*Papio sphinx*) is a species of baboon that lives in the tropical forests of West Africa. Like many forest-dwellers, it is brightly colored so that it can be seen in the leafy gloom. The bright red and blue of a male mandrill's face and rump fade if he is unhealthy, so females can see at a glance whether or not he would make a good mate.

Ischial callosities become red and swollen when female Celebes macaque is in season

SEASONAL SIGNAL
In some primate species, when a female is ready to mate, her rump swells and becomes bright red. This occurs in primates that live in large communities, such as baboons, macaques, and chimpanzees, because more subtle signals might be missed. Primates that pair for life and know each other well, such as gibbons and gorillas, indicate that it is time to mate by more discreet signs, like a slight scent or a change in behavior.

Long tail can be used to waft scent into the air

MESSAGE SCENT
In the lemur world, smell is all-important. A ring-tailed lemur (pp. 10–11) marks its territory with smelly signposts by rubbing scent from its anal gland onto trees and branches. These scent signals announce to other lemurs that another lemur lives in that part of the forest.

MAKING EYES
Monkeys and apes use a range of facial expressions to communicate with each other, which is why they have little fur on their faces and extremely mobile facial muscles. Blinking is used as a mild threat signal in several species, such as this long-tailed macaque (*Macaca fascicularis*), where the signal is heightened by strikingly pale eyelids.

KEEPING IN TOUCH
Touch plays an important role in primate communities. Young primates, such as this bonobo (pp. 56–57), are cradled and protected in their mothers' arms during infancy, and they continue to seek comfort and reassurance through touch all their lives. Chimps and bonobos reinforce social ties by grooming each other, and will often calm tense situations with an encouraging hug, or make peace by offering a friendly hand.

Infant gorilla wanders off to explore

Baby bonobo learns friendly gestures from its mother

White tail tuft stands out in the shady forest

TAIL TAG
Infant gorillas (pp. 48–49) have a white tail tuft until they are about three years old. This shows up on their dark fur like a bull's-eye on a target, acting as a clear visual mark for mother gorillas trying to keep an eye on their youngsters as they play in the shade of the forest vegetation.

On the defense

PRIMATES HAVE MANY predators, but they have developed several ways of avoiding danger. One of the best defenses is living in a group, because there are more pairs of eyes to look out for eagles, snakes, and big cats, as well as for hostile strangers from other groups. Scientists have discovered that some monkeys have a varied vocabulary of danger calls, which are immediately understood by all the other troop members. As soon as a sharp-eyed lookout spots danger, it alerts the rest of the group with a special shriek or chatter, causing the others to run to safety. Larger primates such as gorillas and chimps may stand their ground and try to scare off a predator or a stranger with a threat display.

NEVER SMILE AT A CROCODILE
This 19th-century print of monkeys baiting a crocodile is not as fanciful as it seems. Monkeys do come down to the riverbank occasionally, and they risk their lives – there is a danger of being snapped up by the crocodiles that swiftly swim toward the bank and lunge at the animals drinking there.

ANGER ATTACK
Threats do not come just from predators – they often come from other primates. Apes and monkeys, such as this macaque (pp. 28–29), sometimes lose their tempers. They may vent their anger by shaking and breaking branches. This type of behavior is called "redirected aggression." It allows the angry individual to calm down without resorting to violence against another member of the group.

ON THE BRINK
Fewer sights are more terrifying than a fully grown silverback gorilla (pp. 42–43) about to charge. Gorillas are not naturally aggressive animals, but a silverback will charge, and bite if necessary, any intruder he feels is threatening his troop. The gorilla may also scream, beat his hands on his chest, bare his teeth, and snap branches loudly – behavior calculated to show off his strength and warn off a potential threat.

Eyes seldom stare directly

Lips are tight with annoyance

DROP DEAD
The potto (p. 12) has an unusual defense. When danger threatens, it tucks its head between its forearms, exposing bony vertebral spines to the enemy. If things get serious, the potto has a last resort – it plays dead, dropping from the branch and falling on to the forest floor, cushioned by the soft rainforest leaf litter.

DANGER FROM ABOVE
Monkeys sit and sun themselves or feed in the upper tree branches, making them especially vulnerable to birds of prey. Many birds of prey in tropical rainforests have large talons for crushing monkey skulls – and a deadly habit of gliding silently over the canopy, taking their prey by surprise.

Vervet keeps a wary eye on the skies

From a high vantage point, vervets scan the ground for predators

AIR RAID ALERT
Vervet monkeys (p. 26) live in patches of woodland on the African savanna. If one monkey sees an eagle, it will give a series of low-pitched, short grunts. Any monkey hearing this will quickly head for cover, leaving the branch ends and heading into the thickest part of the foliage. Only a specific call brings this reaction – if a leopard was stalking the monkeys, for example, hiding in branches strong enough to take its weight would be a disaster.

FOLLOW THE CODE
If a vervet monkey gives a short, loud call – a leopard alert – the rest of the troop panics, rushing for the high branches and away from danger. If the call is a high-pitched chatter – an alert for a dangerous snake on the ground – monkeys on the ground stand up and scan the area for a snake in the grass, then run for the trees.

Spotted coat helps camouflage the leopard in shady places

KILLER CAT
The most versatile of the big cats, leopards occupy woodland habitats in places from West Africa to Korea and Southeast Asia. Leopards often relax under shady rocks or lie on branches high in the trees – exactly the places frequented by monkeys and the occasional young ape. Leopards are stealthy and deadly predators, as this unlucky vervet found out.

IT'S A SCREAM
When a chimpanzee is alarmed by a predator, it makes a special expression known as a fear grin (p. 32), pulling back its lips to reveal white teeth and pink gums. If danger is close by, this silent signal warns others without alerting the source of danger. Another option is to make as much noise as possible in order to frighten the predator and alert other chimps.

A leopard kills quickly, with a swift bite to the neck

Hello

Yes

Tickle

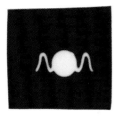

Food

Question

Light

TALKING SYMBOLS
These are some of the "words" in the bonobos' extensive vocabulary.

The great apes

THE FOUR GREAT APES – the chimpanzee, bonobo, gorilla, and orangutan – do not have tails, and they are much larger than prosimians and monkeys. They are also the most intelligent primates apart from humans. Throughout the 20th century, scientists have carried out numerous studies of their behavior and learning abilities, both in captivity and in the wild. The results show that many characteristics that used to be thought of as uniquely human are shared by the great apes as well. We now know that apes can make and use tools (pp. 54–55), solve complex problems, pass on information from one generation to the next, and even learn a language.

Bony crest

BRAIN BOXES
This cross-section of an adult male gorilla skull shows its large braincase. Like humans, the great apes have big, well-developed brains that can store more information than those of other primates. This means that when an ape is faced with a new situation, it has a greater store of knowledge to call upon, offering it a range of possible options.

Ramus bone fits into the temporal bone of the skull

LET YOUR FINGERS DO THE TALKING
Apes will never be able to speak like humans, because their vocal cords cannot produce the necessary range of sounds. But at the Language Research Center in Georgia, scientists have taught pygmy chimps, or bonobos (pp. 56–57), to communicate using sign language. The bonobos understand spoken English but reply to questions and ask for things by pointing to symbols. A bonobo called Kanzi first learned how to "speak" like this, but now others, such as Panbanisha (right), have also mastered the technique.

BOARD TALK
Each of the symbols on this board represents a word. Bonobos like Kanzi have learned several hundred "words" and can combine them to make simple sentences such as "Kanzi tickle." Ape language studies have shown that all four species of great ape can learn sign language, although scientists have yet to find any natural use of language in the wild.

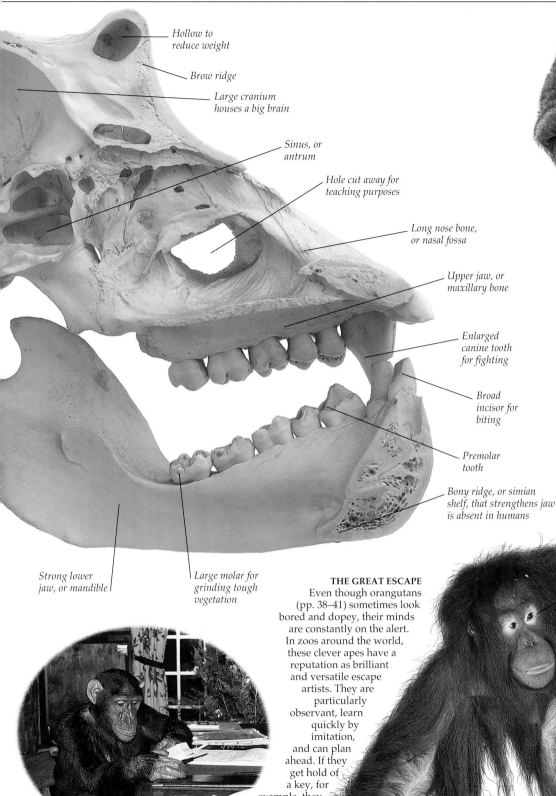

Hollow to reduce weight

Brow ridge

Large cranium houses a big brain

Sinus, or antrum

Hole cut away for teaching purposes

Long nose bone, or nasal fossa

Upper jaw, or maxillary bone

Enlarged canine tooth for fighting

Broad incisor for biting

Premolar tooth

Bony ridge, or simian shelf, that strengthens jaw is absent in humans

Strong lower jaw, or mandible

Large molar for grinding tough vegetation

GIFTED GORILLA
Anyone looking into the eyes of a gorilla can see that there is an intelligent mind looking back. Like chimps, gorillas have shown intelligence and self-awareness in scientific studies. They can recognize themselves on video and are adept at learning sign language. One female lowland gorilla (pp. 44–45) called Koko has become proficient in ASL – American Sign Language for the deaf. She "speaks" with her hands, making signs in rapid succession to form simple sentences.

THE GREAT ESCAPE
Even though orangutans (pp. 38–41) sometimes look bored and dopey, their minds are constantly on the alert. In zoos around the world, these clever apes have a reputation as brilliant and versatile escape artists. They are particularly observant, learn quickly by imitation, and can plan ahead. If they get hold of a key, for example, they might hide it until their keeper is out of sight before trying to undo the lock.

Orang keeps a lookout for the keeper

Strong, nimble fingers can dismantle cage fittings

PROFESSOR CHIMP
Chimps (pp. 50–55), like humans, have an insatiable curiosity. This wild chimpanzee has ventured into a scientists' field camp to carry out a little research! Of all the great apes, chimps and bonobos are considered the most intelligent, and they often show surprisingly original responses to new situations.

The great ape of Asia

ORANGUTANS ARE THE ONLY truly tree-dwelling, or arboreal, great apes. They live deep in the tropical rainforests of Borneo and Sumatra – their name in Malay means "person of the forest." Orangs are shy, solitary animals that rarely come into contact with one another. An adult male roams over a large area of forest and discourages other males from entering his range by occasionally uttering a "long call." Females live apart from males, but their ranges overlap a dominant male's domain. Even when orangutans meet at a feeding site, they seem to ignore one another. But recent research suggests that orangs do know their neighbors, and close relatives sometimes spend time together. However, the number of social interactions seen in one day in a group of chimps (pp. 52–53) might occupy an entire year in an orangutan's social diary.

YOUNG MALE
Between the ages of 10 and 15 years, male orangutans like this one are similar in size and build to females. They become fully mature at about 20 years of age, and only then do they develop a throat pouch and cheek flaps. They also become bulkier and the hair on their shoulders and arms grows longer. Orangutans can live to be 60 years old.

Fatty nodule makes the head look larger

Large body weighs up to 200 lbs (90 kg)

Cheek flap formed from firm, fatty tissue

Cheek flaps on a Bornean male stick out at an angle

Long hair makes the male orang look bigger than he really is

EARLY APE
This 18th-century engraving of an orangutan looks very like a human. Before proper scientific studies of primates were made, there was a great deal of confusion among 18th-century Europeans about the different species of ape. Many weird and wonderful pictures appeared, and all apelike creatures were referred to as orangutans. This orang was kept as a pet by an Englishman, Captain Daniel Beeckman, who visited Borneo in 1712.

FOREST PHANTOM
An adult male orangutan is a strange looking animal. His head is enlarged by two cheek flaps that stick out from either side of his face, and his shoulders are draped in curtains of long hair. Both of these features are designed to make the male look more impressive, because orangutans prefer to settle disputes with a show of strength rather than a fight. When males meet, which is rarely, they stare at each other aggressively, charge around, and shake branches until one of them backs down or they reluctantly fight.

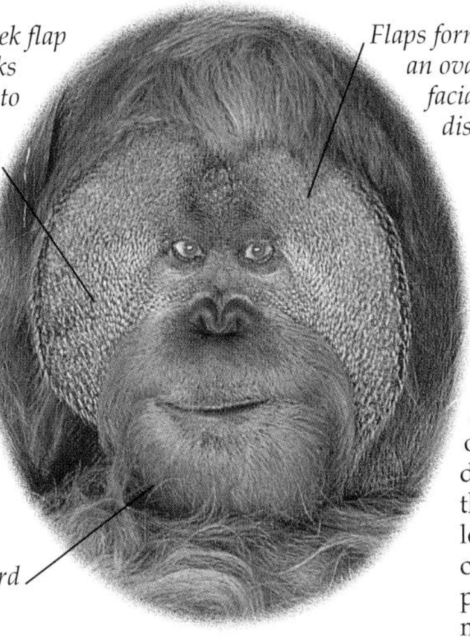

Cheek flap sticks out to the side

Flaps form an oval facial disc

Beard

OLD SUMATRAN

The orangutans of Sumatra (*Pongo pygmaeus abelii*) differ slightly in appearance from their Bornean cousins (*Pongo pygmaeus pygmaeus*). They have lighter-colored hair, and the adult males have flatter-looking cheek flaps and prominent beards.

LONG DISTANCE CALLER

An adult male orangutan develops a large throat pouch that looks like a double chin (right). The pouch enhances the male's "long call," a series of groans and roars that warns nearby males to keep away. The long call carries over half a mile (1 km).

Throat pouch

FRIENDS AND RELATIONS

Unlike most primates, orangs have few opportunities for social grooming because they meet so infrequently. However, siblings or cousins, like these two young females, will sometimes play together and groom each other when they meet with their mothers at a feeding site.

Cheek flaps do not develop in female orangs

Fingers instinctively grasp objects or mother's hair

Mother holds baby protectively in her arms

Female orangutan weighs up to 110 lbs (50 kg)

Hair shorter than that of an adult male

LONE PARENT

Like males, female orangutans lead a largely solitary life, but they usually have one or two offspring with them. Although only one baby is born at a time, a new baby is often born before the older youngster has left the mother. The interval between births is seven or more years, but young orangs are not fully weaned until they are about five years old and they remain with their mother until they are about eight years old. These small single-parent families form the most common social groups in orangutan society.

Forest rangers

ORANGUTANS LOVE fruit. They often range over several square miles or kilometers of rainforest in search of ripe fruit trees. When they find one, orangs do not announce their find to others, but sit quietly eating on their own until they have had their fill. One reason for the orangutan's solitary lifestyle may be its vast appetite. If orangs lived in large groups, they would quickly strip a tree of its fruit, leaving a shortage of food. In tropical forests, fruit trees may grow a long way apart, so eating alone is an advantage for hungry orangs. Some trees bear fruit regularly, but others fruit only once every two or three years. Young orangutans must learn how and where to find food, and they have a long education in jungle living.

CAREFULLY DOES IT
The ability to climb trees only comes with practice to young orangutans, and they are very timid when they first take to the branches.

GETTING THE HANG OF IT
After carefully observing their mothers, then trying it for themselves, young orangs eventually learn to clamber and swing through the trees with confidence.

DOWN TO EARTH
Young orangs are ungainly and vulnerable on the ground, so they rarely descend from the trees. If they do have to walk on the forest floor, they crawl along on half-clenched hands and feet.

Long, strong arms grow to form an armspan of up 8 ft (2.4 m)

HANGING AROUND
Orangutans are extremely versatile climbers. They have strong, hooklike hands and feet and use all four limbs to carry the weight of their bodies. Young orangs are lively and playful and enjoy practicing acrobatic feats in the treetops. However, as they become older and heavier, orangutans begin to move more slowly and spend more time sitting around, snoozing, or simply "hanging out."

LEARNING THE ROPES
Orangutans have the longest childhood of all non-human primates. They stay with their mothers until they are about eight years old. During this time they learn how to survive as they accompany their mothers through the forest. Babies ride on their mothers' backs until they are strong enough to explore nearby trees.

Sweet, waxy flesh

Tough purple skin

MANGOSTEENS
An orangutan uses its big front teeth and strong hands to open tough-skinned fruit such as these mangosteens (*Garcinia mangostana*).

Hard white fruit

Soft spines

Rambutan fruit
(*Nephelium lappaceum*)

Orang dangles on long arms to reach fruit

SKY-WALKER
A heavy orangutan will not normally risk a flying leap between trees. It reaches out for its next hand-hold while keeping a firm grip on a strong branch. If the orang can only reach a thin, leafy branch, it will pull the branch toward it until it can grasp a firmer support. Then the orangutan carefully transfers its weight across the gap to the next tree. Misjudging the strength of a branch 130 ft (40 m) above the ground could prove fatal.

Orang lifts fruit to its mouth with either hands or feet

ORANG NEST
Every night at dusk, an orangutan builds itself a comfortable nest to sleep in. It chooses a suitable tree, preferably with a three-way fork, then weaves together leafy branches to give padding and support.

Hooklike foot is good for grasping branches, but not for walking on the ground

Creamy pulp is highly nutritious

Prickly skin has a strong, fetid odor

PRICKLY PRIZE
Rich in protein and carbohydrates, the prickly durian fruit (*Durio zibethinus*) is a favorite orangutan food. This fruit has a mixed reputation with humans because of its disgusting smell.

Foot used to grip branches or pick fruit

Juvenile female has a full coat of shaggy hair

IT'S RAINING FRUIT
This hard, green fruit looks unappetizing to a young orangutan until it learns how to eat it: first bite off the end, then squeeze the fruit hard between the teeth, and suck out its soft center. With practice, orangutans can pick and eat these fruits so fast that they fall like green hailstones on the forest floor below.

FRUIT EXPERT
By the time an orangutan reaches early maturity, at about the age of 10, it will have learned how to identify over two hundred different food plants. In order to survive in the forest, orangs need to know where to find food, which parts of a fruit are edible, and when different fruit trees are in season. Orangutans appear to carry a "mental map" in their heads of the location of different fruit trees, and when each one is due to bear ripe fruit. They learn this information from their mothers and from their own experience, but they do not share it with others.

King of the apes

YAWNED OFF
A gaping yawn can mean more than a tired gorilla. Gorillas often yawn when nervous. This shows off sharp teeth, warning an aggressor not to disturb or challenge the owner.

W HEN TALK OF A "man-like-monster" first burst upon the scientific world in the middle of the 19th century, it created a sensation. Local people in Africa had lived alongside gorillas for centuries, but their stories were largely dismissed by scientists as travelers' tales. Sadly, for more than a century, the only people who went in search of gorillas were big game hunters looking for trophies. It isn't surprising that they learned mainly about gorilla threat behavior, as the great silverbacks tried in vain to protect their families from the hunters' bullets. Since 1960, however, unarmed field scientists have observed a much gentler side to the greatest of the apes. Their studies have revealed a peaceful vegetarian who likes to lead a quiet life.

STAR OF THE SILVER SCREEN
The movie monster King Kong, seen here fighting off a pterodactyl, was based on popular – and misguided – ideas of the gorilla.

STANDING GUARD
This silverback mountain gorilla (pp. 46–47) is strutting to show off his strength. Adult male gorillas are nearly twice the size of females, because their job is to defend their families from attack. Whatever threatens – be it a leopard, a human hunter, or another, unfriendly, silverback – the leader puts himself between his family and the danger.

Sturdy legs support the massive body weight

SEATED FOR DINNER
Gorillas are vegetarians and they usually eat sitting down. They fold up their short legs, tuck in their feet, and allow their enormous potbellies to protrude between their knees. They can then select food plants growing within reach of their long arms. Once they have eaten all they want from one feeding site, they ease forward onto their knuckles, straighten their legs, and amble on to the next likely-looking clump of plants.

BIG DADDY
The largest primate on earth is the mighty silverback. Adult male gorillas are called silverbacks because of the saddle-shaped area of silvery gray fur that appears when they are about 11 or 12 years old – the age when male gorillas develop the markings of adulthood. As well as a silver back, signs of maturity include a muscular, hairless chest, a crest of bone on the skull, and long shaggy hair on the arms – all designed to make a male look as big as possible. This 19-year-old western lowland silverback (pp. 44–45) weighs more than 400 lbs (180 kg) and stands at a height of 5 ft 10 in (1.78 m).

Powerful neck
muscles give conical
shape to head

Pronounced
brow ridge

Pattern of folds of skin
above the nostrils are
different on every gorilla

Gorilla rests
on knuckles

Big toe can
grasp branches
when climbing

Hair grows on
back of hand to
first knuckle joint

Bony crest

Bony ridge over
eye protects eyeball
from blows

Sharp canine teeth
for tearing food
or fighting

Broad incisor teeth
for grinding food

Strong jaw

BONEHEAD
A silverback's skull is strong and well-protected.
The heavy jaw is powered by enormous muscles
attached to a bony crest on top of the head.

KING OF THE JUNGLE
The male gorilla is famous
for his chest-beating display,
which is used to intimidate
rivals or to impress females.
During the display, the
gorilla gives a series of
hoots, before rising to his
feet and beating his chest
with cupped hands (not
clenched fists), making
a "pok-pok-pok" sound.
He then charges
forwards, first on two
legs, then on all fours,
before thumping the
ground with his hands.

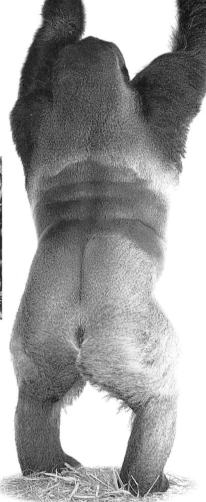

TOWER OF STRENGTH
Although gorillas are mainly
quadrupedal (p. 9), they will often stand
upright to reach up for something, to look
over the top of thick vegetation, or to beat
their chests. A silverback on his hind legs
can measure up to 6 ft 7in (2 m) tall – a
sight calculated to scare off any potential
enemies. The vast, rippling muscles on
this silverback add to his stature.

43

Gorilla family life

WESTERN LOWLAND GORILLAS (*Gorilla gorilla gorilla*) have to work harder for their food than their mountain cousins (pp. 46–47). They live in tropical rainforests, where there are fewer nutritious plants at ground level than in the more open mountain woodlands. This means that lowland gorillas may have to travel long distances in order to find food. Their day begins just after dawn, when they rise and set off through the forest. The gorillas eat as they walk along, but if they find a ripe fruit tree, they will clamber into the branches to consume the fruit. Once they are full, the gorillas build day-nests on the ground in which to sleep off their exertions. After two or three hours' rest, the troop moves off again into the forest and travels until dusk, snacking on plants along the way. When the silverback leader decides it is time to stop, each gorilla builds a new nest and settles down for the night.

HIGH CLIMBER
This young zoo gorilla is playing on a climbing frame. For many years, scientists thought that gorillas were too heavy to climb trees, until they studied them in the wild. They found that even adults are surprisingly agile and often climb high into trees to reach ripe fruit.

19th-century engraving of a gorilla family

White tail tuft helps mother locate infant in the jungle

A QUICK BITE
Gorillas sometimes crouch on two feet like this to gather up fallen fruit, or when there is not enough food in one place to make it worth sitting down! It is also a useful posture to adopt when feeding on fierce soldier ants, because it exposes less of the body to their painful stings.

Juvenile has lost its white tail tuft

Nimble fingers pick up fruit

TIME TO GO
A western lowland gorilla troop is usually made up of about 5 to 15 animals. Apart from the silverback, it may include one or two young adult males, several adult females, and a number of juveniles and infants. Females such as this one may leave their parents' group and join another group to avoid inbreeding.

Weight rests on the knuckles while walking

A SLIMMER GORILLA

In the gorilla world, it is not unhealthy to have a potbelly. It just means that the owner eats a hearty diet of bulky vegetation. Many zoo gorillas (right) look much slimmer than those in the wild because they are often fed on pellets of concentrated food, and given fewer fruits and vegetables.

LIFE AT THE TOP

The big silverback is lord of all he surveys. Apart from making all the day-to-day decisions for the troop, he can also take his pick of the breeding females. Serious fights among male gorillas are infrequent, but the silverback may take exception to another male when he becomes fully mature at about 11 or 12 years. The younger male may decide to leave the troop, and he will live alone or with other males until he can form his own troop.

Bare chest is a sign of maturity

Young gorilla can watch the world go by from its safe perch

JUNGLE EXPLORER

A young gorilla learns to walk at about five to six months. When it is 18 months, like this young gorilla, it can follow its mother on foot for short distances, often resting one hand on her rump for security. By the time it is two, it has enough confidence to follow the troop on its own. However, the young gorilla stays close to its mother so it can climb on her back if it gets scared or tired.

Mother munches as she walks along

Gorilla leans forward to use his teeth on a stubborn plant

ON THE MOVE

The safest place for a young gorilla traveling through the jungle is on its mother's back. From here it can watch the other members of the troop as they follow the broad silvery back of the dominant male along the forest floor. Infant gorillas depend upon their mothers for transport until they are about two and a half or three years old, by which time they are strong enough to walk by themselves for fairly long distances.

Food picked from the wayside

Pot belly

BREAKFAST IN BED

If food is within easy reach when a gorilla wakes up in its night-nest, it will have breakfast in bed before setting off into the forest. The silverback decides the pace and direction of the day's travel and will also indicate when it is time to stop and rest. Although he may look easygoing, the silverback keeps a constant lookout for possible dangers along the way.

The mountain gorillas

LIFE FOR MOUNTAIN GORILLAS (*Gorilla gorilla beringei*) is rather like being on a never-ending picnic where leisurely eating is only interrupted by playing, exploring, sleeping, and the occasional downpour. These easygoing apes have become the focus of many scientific studies because they seem to be less afraid of humans than their lowland cousins, and they are relatively easy to follow in their woodland habitat. However, the peaceful existence of the mountain gorillas is threatened. Due to hunting, loss of habitat, and war, they have become one of the world's most endangered mammals. In 1925 their home in the mountain forests of the Virunga Volcanoes was declared Africa's first national park. Today there are fewer than 650 mountain gorillas left in the world.

GORILLA GUARDIAN
The late Dr. Dian Fossey (1932–1985) is one of the best known gorilla researchers. She won the trust of mountain gorillas by learning to imitate their sounds and gestures. These two orphaned baby gorillas, which she nursed back to health after poachers killed their parents, taught her some of the soft sounds of contented gorillas. She was then able to reassure frightened wild gorillas by speaking to them in their own "language."

VANTAGE POINT
Gorillas spend most of their time on the ground, but will often climb trees to search for fruit, bark, or leaves – or just to see further.

Thick, shaggy fur keeps out the chilling rain

Play-fights may look fierce, but they rarely result in injury

ROUGH-AND-TUMBLE
Just like human children, young gorillas spend much of their time playing and getting to know one another. Games of follow-the-leader, tag, or simply good-natured play-fighting all help to develop a youngster's strength and coordination.

GORILLAS IN THE DOWNPOUR
The mist of Dian Fossey's famous book, *Gorillas in the Mist*, often turns to rain. Caught in a downpour at an altitude of 10,000 ft (3,000 m), there is not much this gorilla can do, other than sit very still and wait for the rain to end. His thick fur keeps out the chill, while water runs off the outer layer of hairs. Mothers wrap their shaggy arms around their babies to keep them warm and dry.

Bramble
(*Rubus* sp.)

*Gorillas eat
both the leaves
and berries*

Wild celery
(*Peucedanum* sp.)

Dock leaves
(*Rumex* sp.)

*Gorillas
eat only
the roots*

Woody flesh

Bracket fungus
(*Canoderma* sp.)

HOW TO EAT
Gorillas are fussy eaters, taking care
that each mouthful is prepared
exactly how they like it. They select,
pick, and prepare their food plants
fresh from the ground. This
adult female has just
pulled up and peeled
a long, crunchy,
hollow stem of
wild celery.

DAILY DIET
Mountain gorillas
don't have to go far for
their food. The cool, rainy
mountain weather encourages
the growth of dense vegetation,
which means that the gorillas are
surrounded by food. Much of a gorilla's
daily diet is made up of bedstraw, wild
celery, nettles, and thistles. Special treats are
bamboo, bracket fungus, or a bramble bush.

*Female snoozes
in a comfortable
day-nest*

AFTER-DINNER NAP
At dusk, after the late
afternoon feeding
session, gorillas usually
build a nest on the
ground. Each gorilla
over the age of four
makes its own nest –
a new one every night –
where it sleeps until
morning. Gorillas make
smaller day-nests after
the late morning feed,
in which they spend
the midday siesta,
dozing in the sun –
or huddled in the rain.

*Companionable
gorillas sit
close together*

*Young gorilla
clambers playfully
over an adult*

PLAYING WITH THE YOUNG ONES
When gorillas are foraging for food,
they spread out to avoid arguments
over particularly choice food plants.
But by late morning, when they
are full, they settle down for a
rest. This is the time for
socializing, grooming,
and playing with the
young ones – in fact, it
is not uncommon to see
a good-natured silverback
being beaten up or jumped
upon by a toddler.

Devoted parents

Primates are excellent parents. Most have only one baby at a time, and one or both parents will take great care of it until it is old enough to look after itself. Like all newborn primates, a baby gorilla is tiny and helpless. It is totally dependent on its mother for warmth, food, and protection. The young gorilla feeds on its mother's milk until it is fully weaned at about two years of age, although it begins to eat solid food by about six months. A gorilla has a long childhood because it must learn how to survive in the wild and how to live in a social group. It stays close to its mother, sleeping in her nest until it is three or four, when it becomes an independent member of the gorilla troop. Even after that, a juvenile gorilla often returns to its mother for protection and support.

ROCK-A-BYE BABY
A loving gorilla mother often cradles her baby in her arms even though a newborn infant can cling to its mother's fur without her help. At first, the baby hangs on to its mother's chest, but it soon learns how to ride around on her back.

Spine

Pelvis

Pregnant female near the end of her gestation period

Long bone of upper leg, or femur

Main shin bone, or tibia

Lesser shin bone, or fibula

HIDDEN BULGE
A female gorilla's gestation period – the time between mating and birth – lasts about eight and a half months. It is often difficult to spot a pregnant female, because a gorilla's diet of bulky, fibrous vegetation means her belly is usually well developed even before she becomes pregnant. Female gorillas are ready to breed at about eight years of age.

Tarsal and metatarsal bones of foot

Fetus at eight months

Umbilical cord

Placenta transfers food and oxygen to baby's blood

Powerful neck
muscles

Shoulder blade,
or scapula

Eyes protected
by ridge of bone

Female has
smaller incisor
teeth than male

Powerful jaw
juts forward

Mastoid muscle
to power jaw

Mobile shoulder joint
allows arm to be raised
for tree-climbing

Heart

Rib cage
protects heart
and lungs in
thoracic cavity

Long bone of
the upper arm,
or humerus

Lungs

Liver

Outer bone of the
forearm, or radius

Inner bone of the
forearm, or ulna

Abdominal
cavity contains
main organs of
digestive and
reproductive
systems

GORILLA TODDLER
By five or six months, as an infant
gorilla gains strength and coordination,
it begins to crawl clumsily from its
mother's lap while she rests or feeds.
The time spent away from the mother
increases with confidence – young
gorillas of a similar age will usually
find each other for games of chase
or bouts of wrestling.

Carpal and
metacarpal
bones of
the hand

BENEATH THE SKIN
This cross-section model of a pregnant gorilla
shows the fetus inside the womb just before the
end of the gestation period. When a baby gorilla
is born, it weighs about 4–6 lbs (2–3 kg) – only
half the size of a human baby. The baby's pink
skin darkens a few days after birth, and its thin
fur begins to grow thicker. Female gorillas give
birth about once every four years.

The chimpanzee

CHIMPANZEES ARE MANY PEOPLE'S favorite great apes, but they are not the cuddly creatures often portrayed in the media. Wild chimps are intelligent, powerful animals that live in complex communities (pp. 52–53). They often work together to hunt other animals, and they have even been known to wage war on their own kind. Chimps are incredibly smart. They have developed a remarkable range of tool-using skills (pp. 54–55), and have been able to adapt to both forest and savanna regions in western and central Africa. But part of what makes chimpanzees so fascinating is their close relationship to humans. Not only do they look like us, but they often seem to behave like us as well.

MISTAKEN IDENTITY
Chimpanzees are prone to baldness, which led to some confusion in the past. When a bald chimp was spotted by the 19th-century hunter Paul du Chaillu (p. 62), he thought it was a new species and called it the "koola-kamba."

FACE FACTS
Common chimps have many facial colorations. The eastern race (*Pan troglodytes schweinfurthii*) has a pink face when young, and the western race (*Pan troglodytes verus*) has a dark mask around the eyes, but there is a great deal of individual variation.

Large ears can pick up the calls of other chimps in the forest

Like other primates, chimps have color vision for spotting ripe fruit

EYE-TO-EYE
Chimpanzees have hairy foreheads and bare brows. In humans, this arrangement is reversed, but both patterns draw attention to the eyes. Like humans, chimps have expressive faces which are used for communication, and eyes for sending out all-important signals.

Large braincase

Long canine of adult male

BIG HEAD
Although a chimpanzee's skull is very sturdy, with a strong jaw and a protective bony ring around the eyes, it is not as powerfully built as a gorilla's (p. 43). Nevertheless, the chimp's thinner skull houses a much bigger brain in comparison to its body size.

Strong jaw

Long muzzle

Broad incisors for biting into fruit

Adult male weighs up to 110 lbs (50 kg) and is seven times stronger than a man

THEM AND US
Resting on its haunches with its hands on its knees, this chimp looks almost human. Recent research suggests that chimpanzees and bonobos (pp. 56–57), are actually more closely related to humans than to other apes. Some of their expressions and gestures certainly seem to reflect our own, but it is important not to interpret their behavior according to ours. Many expressions, such as grinning (p. 32), have completely different meanings in chimp society.

Eyes have a pleading look

Chimp squeezes fruit to test ripeness

Hand held out for food

Weight rests on knuckles (p. 9)

BREAKFAST IN THE BRANCHES
Chimps spend a lot of time in the trees searching for fruit, which makes up the bulk of their diet. They are adept climbers and can swing from both arms like gibbons (pp. 30–31), although they cannot travel like this for long distances. Chimps often cover up to 4 mi (6.4 km) a day in search of food, mostly walking on the ground.

Baby chimps are born with pink skin

ELDER STATESMAN
Chimpanzees can live to the age of 50. In the chimp community (pp. 52–53), older members are treated with respect, even though they are not as strong as they used to be. Younger chimps often groom them and share food treats with them, such as meat or rare fruit. This old male is holding out his hand beseechingly for a morsel of food.

WATCH WITH MOTHER
Like the other great apes, chimpanzees have long childhoods during which they learn the social rules of their communities and how to survive in the forest. A young chimp is completely dependent on its mother until it is about five years old, and even after it becomes fully mature at around 13, it spends a great deal of time with her.

Young chimp practices making a nest by bending leafy branches into a comfortable platform

PRACTICE MAKES PERFECT
Chimpanzees learn how to fend for themselves by watching and copying their mothers. For example, every night a young chimp watches its mother making a nest for them both in a tree. It will then play at nest building, developing its technique and learning how to pick the best nest sites. When its mother has another baby, usually after about five years, the young chimp will be forced to make its own sleeping arrangements.

The ape extrovert

CHIMPANZEES ARE HIGHLY SOCIABLE animals that live in large communities of 80 or more members. They do not stay together all the time, but form small foraging parties that wander along known trails in their home range. A chimp may spend an entire day alone, or meet and mingle with a number of others throughout the day, first tagging along with one group and then another. When two groups meet, there is a great deal of noise and excitement. Friends and relatives greet each other with hooting, hugging, and back-patting, while rivals approach more warily. Chimp society is incredibly complex and has a constantly changing hierarchy. It is important for a chimpanzee to know who are the dominant individuals and to treat them with respect. Chimps also learn how to gauge each other's feelings by reading the subtle signals sent out by sounds, facial expressions, and posture.

FOOD ALERT!
Loud, excited hoots echo through the forest when a chimpanzee finds a wild fig tree laden with fruit. Any other chimps within earshot will head straight for the tree to share in the feast. A chimp is happy to share such a find, because it may benefit from someone else's discovery on another day.

FINDING A HOME
A young chimp mother will usually establish herself in the same area as her mother, providing there is plenty of food. She must be respectful to dominant females who already live there, but once she has gained acceptance, she may team up with other mothers to form a "nursery" group. Female chimps rise in rank as they become older and have more children.

Female defers to dominant male

Dominant male is center of attention

GROUP POWWOW
In male chimp society, rank depends as much on brains and personality as on strength. However, a high-ranking male still needs a group of supporters, and he must work hard to maintain their loyalty. A dominant male will make friends with one or two other males, who then spend all their time with him, backing him up in disputes if necessary. Other chimps form rival gangs, but although there are constant power plays and confrontations, opposing groups often team up for long grooming sessions to maintain peaceful relations.

FAVORITE PREY
Chimpanzees eat meat as well as fruit and plants, and red colobus monkeys (above) are one of their favorite prey. Chimps are clever and deadly predators, often banding together in hunting parties to catch monkeys, small antelopes, and bush pigs.

LET'S MAKE FRIENDS
After an unsuccessful challenge to a dominant male, a low-ranking chimp adopts a submissive posture by crouching with his back to his superior. The dominant male (on the right) reassures his subordinate by gently touching him on the back. These gestures are also common when high-rank and low-rank chimps greet each other.

PLAY TIME
Young chimps receive most of their food from their mothers' milk, so they have a lot of free time for playing. They spend most of the day chasing and wrestling, climbing and swinging, building up their muscles and learning the rules of chimpanzee society.

AFTER THE HUNT
This successful hunter is eating monkey meat with leaves. West African chimps catch colobus monkeys in high-speed chases involving an amazing degree of group coordination. Once they have spotted monkeys in the trees, some members of the hunting party form an ambush while others herd the monkeys into the trap. However, in Tanzania, chimps usually hunt alone by stealthily creeping up on a monkey and grabbing it. When a monkey is caught, it is greedily torn limb from limb.

YOU SCRATCH MY BACK, AND I'LL SCRATCH YOURS
Grooming is one of the most important activities in chimpanzee social life. Through grooming, chimps strengthen friendships and family ties and patch up old disagreements. A chimp will work intently, combing another's fur with its fingers, carefully picking out dirt, twigs, and lice, and cleaning cuts and scratches. A grooming session usually lasts up to an hour, but if more chimps join in, it can last longer.

Hair stands on end to make the chimp look threatening

Younger chimp sees dominant male as his role model

SQUARING UP
Unlike macaque society (p. 29), rank in a chimpanzee community is not inherited from parents. There is a constantly changing hierarchy among group members, which leads to frequent disputes such as this one. Like saloon bar brawlers, these two chimps trade threats while sizing each other up. The younger male on the left is building up his confidence with a series of pants and hoots, but the larger, more confident male stands ready for any move. Many duels like this are settled with threat displays and never come to blows.

The great engineer

CLEAR OFF!
Chimps often use branches and rocks as make shift weapons to throw at predators or rival groups of chimps.

CHIMPANZEES ARE THE ENGINEERS of the non-human primate world. They are highly skilled at making and using a wide variety of tools, which they use for a number of different tasks. Although other animals use tools, they are less versatile than chimps. Chimpanzees carefully select, prepare, and adapt their tools to suit a particular purpose, and they have been known to plan ahead by carrying tools with them to a special site. Their main implements are sticks and stones. Sticks are used to probe insect nests or to test something the chimp is unsure about; stones are employed as hammers to crack open nuts or as missiles to hurl at predators and rivals. Chimpanzees often use bundles of leaves to keep themselves clean, wiping dirt from their fur or sticky fruit juice from their fingers. They have also been seen using twigs to pick bits of food from their teeth or even to ease out a rotting tooth.

LEAF SPONGE
Chimps have learned how to drink rainwater from tree holes by using a wad of leaves to mop it up. Experienced chimps will chew the leaves first to make the leaf sponge more absorbent.

HANDY HINTS
It is the combination of strong, precise fingers and an inventive mind that makes chimps such good designers and users of tools. These are the very qualities that lie behind the success of the human species, which is why scientists are particularly interested in chimpanzees' tool-using abilities.

Strong hand grips coconut firmly

Chimp probing with a stick

ROCK BOTTOM
This chimpanzee is using the rocks on the bottom of a stream as an anvil on which to bash a hard coconut. Chimps are not afraid of water, and young chimps have sometimes been seen holding a stick into a swirling stream, apparently in order to watch the ripples flowing around it.

CLEVER STICKS
Chimpanzees use sticks for numerous purposes. They are used most often to break open insect nests such as underground bees' nests, or to investigate holes in trees. A chimp will often insert a stick into an opening, then draw it out and sniff it to find out what's inside.

Chimp strips the bark off rod with its teeth

Unlike other animals, chimps can concentrate on a task for hours

Infant watches and learns from its mother

MAKING A ROD
Chimpanzees love to eat ants and termites, but they are often difficult to extract from their nests and mounds. However, a peeled twig or a palm frond makes an excellent insect fishing rod.

GONE FISHING
A chimp will often spend up to three hours fishing for termites. Once it has made a rod, it gently inserts it into the narrow tunnels of a termite mound. When the termites attack the rod with their pincers, the chimp carefully pulls it out, with termites attached, to inspect its catch.

TERMITE TREAT
Eating termites can be a risky business. They must be sucked quickly off the fishing rod and crunched up before they can bite. Scientists who tried to fish for termites themselves discovered that it is much harder than it looks. Youngsters learn by watching their mothers and then practicing on their own.

ROCK HAMMER
In West Africa, chimpanzees have learned how to use stone hammers and wooden clubs to crack open nuts against rocks or the flat roots of trees. This is a highly skilled job. A nut must be struck hard enough to break the shell, but not so hard as to crush the nutritious kernel. Adult females seem to be the best nut-crackers and they teach their skills to their offspring.

Younger chimp waits to receive a tasty nut

Rock hammer can weigh up to 20 lbs (9 kg)

The fourth great ape

DEEP IN THE REMOTE RAINFORESTS of central Zaire, Africa, lives the least known of the great apes – the bonobo, or pygmy chimpanzee (*Pan paniscus*). Bonobos were the last of the four great apes to be formally identified by scientists in 1929. Before that, they were thought to be just another kind of common chimpanzee (pp. 50–51). Although they are sometimes called pygmy chimps, bonobos are about the same size as common chimpanzees, but they have smaller heads and more slender, graceful bodies. Bonobos and common chimps share similar lifestyles with one or two major differences. Bonobos spend more time in the trees, and they form closer-knit communities in which the females play a more dominant role.

Baldness is common in captive apes

PROUD MATRIARCH
This female bonobo from the San Diego Zoo is called Lana. She is famous for her intelligence and skill as a mother. In bonobo society, females form the stable core of the group, unlike common chimp society, where the males are more assertive (pp. 52–53).

Slender arms and narrow shoulders make bonobos look lean and lanky

Silky black coat

FINE FEATURES
It is easy to tell a bonobo from a common chimpanzee. The bonobo has a neat parting on the skull and hair which falls down on both sides of the face. It also has a slightly smaller head, a dark face, and red lips.

BEST FRIENDS

Bonobos are intensely sociable animals. Adult female bonobos form strong friendships, which are reinforced by social behavior such as embracing and mutual grooming.

MATERNAL GUIDANCE

This baby is learning from its mother how to recognize one of the bonobos' 300 or so food plants, and which parts of the plant are edible. Although fruit, leaves, stems, and pith form the bulk of their diet, bonobos sometimes prey on baby duikers (small forest antelopes).

Playing in the trees strengthens muscles and improves coordination

LITTLE MEN

Judging from contemporary drawings, the first ape to be brought to Europe in the 17th century was probably a bonobo. The appearance of apes created a great deal of confusion – some scientists thought they were the legendary pygmy people of Africa!

CHILD'S PLAY

Bonobos are very affectionate. They will often use sex and touch to calm themselves down during an exciting or tense situation, such as finding a new food supply or meeting another group. Even youngsters like these display this kind of behavior.

Characteristic hair parting

CLIMBING HIGH

High up a tree, a young bonobo chews happily on a branch. Bonobos spend much of their day feeding in the treetops, and the bulk of their diet is made up of fruit.

Lean, lithe body

Young bonobo gets a hand-up from its mother

JUNGLE GYM

A springy branch or palm frond makes a perfect bouncy climbing frame for a young bonobo. Adult bonobos may join in, and play can often become quite boisterous. Bonobos are not much lighter than chimpanzees – males average 100 lbs (45 kg), females 73 lbs (33 kg), but they are extremely lithe and spend much more time in the trees than common chimpanzees.

Monkey myths

For thousands of years, people have told stories about monkeys and apes. They are featured as both heroes and villains in countless folk tales and even play a role in some religions. In medieval church carvings, monkeys were often used to depict the devil, but in Buddhist and Hindu mythology, monkeys are seen as wise and brave. The ancient Egyptians worshiped the regal-looking hamadryas baboon (p. 26) as a sacred animal and encouraged baboons to live in temples, embalming their bodies when they died. In India, where monkeys are revered perhaps more than anywhere else in the world, hanuman langurs (*Presbytis entellus*) still enjoy a sacred status. They are allowed to roam around villages and towns, or even to raid crops, without being chased away.

A NOBLE POSE
With its impressive cloak of gray fur and regal sitting pose, the male hamadryas baboon lives up to its sacred status. Egyptian gods were often shown with baboon features and sitting in the same dignified position.

TEACHING TRIO
Perhaps the most famous primates in the world are the Japanese three wise monkeys, "Hear-no-evil, See-no-evil, Speak-no-evil." Based on Japanese macaques (p. 29), they were once used to teach Buddhist doctrine.

Engraved orangutan skulls are often used in funeral ceremonies

MONKEY HERO
"Monkey" is the hero of a famous Chinese novel written during the Ming dynasty (1368–1580). He accompanied a monk, Hsuan Tsang, and two other animals, Pigsy and Sandy, on an epic 17-year journey. Monkey is said to have hatched from a stone egg, but this Chinese monkey is carved in jade.

SACRED SKULL
The Dayak people of Borneo worship orangutans (pp. 38–41) as their ancestral spirits.

ROCK OF THE APES
When the British arrived in Gibraltar, on the tip of the Spanish peninsula, in 1704, they adopted as lucky mascots the troop of Barbary macaques (*Macaca sylvanus*), mistakenly known as apes, which had settled there. It is said that the apes once warned the garrison of a Spanish invasion, and so they came to symbolize the strength of the British. During World War II, when Gibraltar became a place of strategic importance, the British prime minister, Winston Churchill (1874–1965) ordered that the apes be restocked, to ensure that the territory remained in British hands. The macaques' descendants are still in residence today.

NOT YETI DISCOVERED

In 1899 a British officer in the Himalayas reported finding footprints of "the strange hairy wild men who are believed to live among the eternal snows." This began the world's fascination with the yeti, or as the press called it, the "abominable snowman." In remote parts of North America such mysterious tracks are attributed to "big-foot." If evidence is ever found to prove that either creature exists, it is unlikely to look like this fanciful monster.

LITTLE-FOOT

In the forests of Sumatra, zoologists have found primate tracks that they find deeply puzzling. They seem to belong to a small apelike creature that walks on two legs. For the local people there is no mystery – they call the owner of the tracks "orang pendek," or "short person." This unknown primate has been described as a small, graceful gorilla-like animal with golden brown fur, which is no more than 4 ft (1.2 m) tall.

Plaster cast of an orang pendek's footprint taken in 1994

GOOD DEED

Hindus believe that the monkey god Hanuman, shown on this 18th-century bronze plaque from southern India, is the ancestor of all monkeys. According to legend, Hanuman and his monkey followers helped the god Rama to recapture his wife Sita from the island of Sri Lanka by building a causeway with boulders carried down from the Himalayas.

Hanuman has monkey features and a human body

BURNT FINGERS

The air around the monkey temple at Benares in India is alive with the screechings of its most famous residents – hundreds of sacred hanuman langurs. Hindu legend tells how the langurs got their black hands and faces: a langur was caught stealing mangoes from a giant's garden in Sri Lanka to give to the people of Bengal. As a punishment, the giant set his tail alight, but the brave langur survived. Only his face and hands were burned, and all his ancestors still have the same markings.

People and primates

APES, MONKEYS, AND HUMANS have often had an uneasy relationship. People have frequently treated their primate relatives as playthings or curiosities, and this is still the case in some parts of the world today. But thanks to the work of a number of dedicated scientists and organizations, attitudes towards primates are slowly changing. Many countries are clamping down on the export of primates for the pet trade, and special sanctuaries have been set up to care for primate orphans. Most good zoos now house their primates in roomy, tree-filled enclosures, giving people the opportunity to meet a family of gorillas or a troop of monkeys in an almost natural setting, and primate research centers are helping to increase our knowledge and understanding of our closest animal relatives.

PART OF THE FAMILY
Monkeys have lived alongside humans for centuries. This family seems to have a pet monkey as well as a dog.

LIVING DOLL
In 18th-century Europe and America, pet monkeys and marmosets (pp. 14–15), dressed as miniature people, became all the rage among members of the aristocracy. Because people knew little about primate needs, their pets usually died before reaching maturity. Nevertheless, many monkeys were so loved that grieving owners had their dead pets stuffed and displayed at home.

CROWD PULLER
Even at the beginning of the 20th century, monkeys were such an unusual sight that people would crowd around to see one. Barrel organs were commonplace in the streets of many European cities – so to attract the crowds, musicians used a dressed-up monkey to pass a hat around for coins.

Scientists spend many hours in the forest collecting data

Mountain gorillas have become used to human observers

GORILLA WATCH
The work of Dr. Dian Fossey (p. 46) has been continued by many other scientists since her death in 1985. Using the techniques she developed, such as crouching and making reassuring gorilla noises, they continue to study and protect the 650 mountain gorillas that are left. Small parties of tourists can now also enjoy a gorilla encounter in Zaire and Uganda. Furthermore, park fees and hotels have brought money and jobs to the local people, contributing to the development of the region. Similar programs now play a role in chimpanzee and orangutan conservation.

THE FIRST PRIMATE IN SPACE
Because of their similarity to humans, apes and monkeys have often been used as human stand-ins for scientific experiments. In January 1961, a three-year-old chimpanzee called Ham was secured inside a space capsule and sent on a 16-minute space voyage. He was monitored throughout the trip by a camera, which relayed his every reaction to anxious human observers on the ground. Ham survived his 5000-mph (8045-kph) trip and became an instant celebrity. His voyage, and those of many other chimponauts, paved the way for the first human space flights.

COCONUT COLLECTOR
In Sumatra, local people have trained pig-tailed macaques (p. 29) to collect coconuts. The agile macaques scramble up the slender coconut trees and twist the coconuts from the top, dropping the heavy nuts down to their human partners waiting below. People can also scale coconut trees, but macaques are much better climbers!

FINDING A SANCTUARY
Misguided love of baby apes and monkeys is threatening their very survival. Many are taken from the wild illegally to be sold into the pet trade, often after their mothers have been shot. Those that are rescued are placed in special sanctuaries like this one in Africa. These chimp orphans are learning how to behave like wild chimpanzees from their human teacher.

FOSTER FAMILY.
At the Yerkes Regional Primate Research Center in Georgia, many chimpanzees are reared in captivity. Although young chimps have needs similar to those of human children, it is important that they not be raised as humans, because they must learn how to fit into chimp society. By carefully studying and then copying the behavior of mother chimpanzees, the staff at Yerkes are learning how to raise orphan chimps as they would be raised by their own mothers.

Human foster parent mimicks the behavior of a mother chimp

Young chimps love being tickled

Baby chimps need as much care and attention as human babies

Primates in danger

Rwandan machete, or umuhuru, used by both poachers and rangers to cut trails in the forest

THE LOSS OF HABITAT is the single greatest threat to non-human primates. As the human population continues to rise, more and more areas of forest are being cut down for timber or cleared for farmland. Apart from the destruction of their homes, primates are also threatened by hunters. Killed for their meat and skins, or to provide young primates for medical research or the pet trade, some species are on the brink of extinction. Many countries have passed laws banning the hunting of endangered primates and have set aside national parks to preserve what is left of their habitats. For some primates, breeding in captivity is improving their chances of survival. A growing number of zoos and animal parks are breeding primates in the hope that some can be reintroduced to their natural homes.

TROPHY HUNTER
American hunter Paul du Chaillu's (1835–93) account of hunting gorillas in the 1860s created a sensation. His description of the great African gorillas encouraged others to go in search of the ultimate trophy.

Spearhead probably hammered from scrap metal

Metal point on end of spear to balance the spearhead

Hardwood shaft

BANK-ROLLING THE GORILLAS
Gorilla tourism (p. 60) in Rwanda was so successful that the government put gorillas on banknotes as a sign of their value.

NATIONAL TREASURE
Kings, queens, presidents, and generals have appeared on bank notes, but Mahashe (above) is the only named gorilla. This impressive silverback is the leader of a gorilla family in Kahuzi-Biega National Park, Zaire, where he won fame for his size, strength, and gentle disposition.

POACHER'S KIT
Hunters who ignore the boundaries of national parks and continue to kill endangered species are called poachers. Some commercial poachers use shotguns, rifles, or even machine guns to kill their prey. Others may follow traditional hunting practices, using homemade spears and arrows like these.

A SECOND CHANCE
Poachers often shoot mother orangutans in order to sell their babies as pets. Rescued baby orangs are sent to centers where they are cared for until they are old enough to be returned to the wild. The orangutans are taught how to fend for themselves in the forest, but feeding stations such as this one provide newly returned orangs with a food supply for as long as they need it.

BURNING ISSUE
The greatest threat to primates is the loss of their forest homes. Since the 1940s, more than half of the world's tropical rainforests have been destroyed by human activities. Trees are felled for timber or to clear land for ranches, small farms, and plantations. Once the big trees have gone, the bushes and cut branches are usually burned. Many animals die in the flames or are shot as they flee from the fire. The development of farming methods that require less land is vital if the world's rainforests, and the animals that live in them, are to survive.

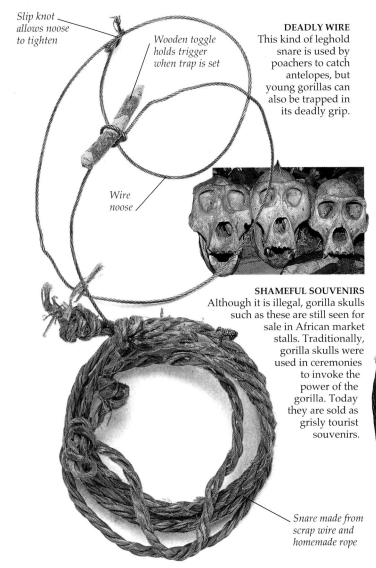

Slip knot allows noose to tighten

Wooden toggle holds trigger when trap is set

DEADLY WIRE
This kind of leghold snare is used by poachers to catch antelopes, but young gorillas can also be trapped in its deadly grip.

Wire noose

WILDLIFE POLICE
Many national parks have special anti-poaching patrols like this one in the Virunga Volcanoes, Rwanda. The patrollers destroy poachers' snares and sometimes catch poachers red-handed.

SHAMEFUL SOUVENIRS
Although it is illegal, gorilla skulls such as these are still seen for sale in African market stalls. Traditionally, gorilla skulls were used in ceremonies to invoke the power of the gorilla. Today they are sold as grisly tourist souvenirs.

HIDDEN DANGER
Concealed in the undergrowth, poachers' snares pose a serious threat to great apes. Although they are not the poachers' most common targets, gorillas are still hunted illegally in some African countries for "bush meat" or for their hands, feet, and skulls, which are sold as traditional charms or to tourists.

Big wire noose strong enough to trap even a silverback gorilla

Snare made from scrap wire and homemade rope